PARADISE:

THE

PLACE AND STATE OF SAVED SOULS

BETWEEN

DEATH AND THE RESURRECTION.

BY

ROBERT M. PATTERSON,
PHILADELPHIA.

"*To-day shalt thou be with me in paradise.*"

PHILADELPHIA:
PRESBYTERIAN BOARD OF PUBLICATION,
1334 CHESTNUT STREET.

WESTCOTT & THOMSON,
Stereotypers and Electrotypers, Phila.

CONTENTS.

PARADISE.

CHAPTER I.

INTRODUCTORY.—THE SUBJECT AND ITS IMPORTANCE.

HERE is the abode, and what is the state, of saved souls between the death and the resurrection of their bodies?

This question is one of immediate and practical interest to Christians. It is of immediate interest because death is ever at their door. To-morrow, to-night, it may seize them; and then where do they go? It is not merely of speculative but of intense practical interest, for true views of it should minister to their comfort and increase their faithfulness in this life.

"When our friends leave us for a foreign country to take up their residence there," says a thoughtful theologian, "our thoughts and our affections naturally follow them; and the questions often suggest themselves to our minds, Where are they, and how are they engaged? What are their circumstances? What are their employments? What are their prospects? This current of thought and feeling acquires additional depth and fullness and force if it be certain, or even probable, that we shall sooner or later follow them to the distant land to which they have migrated. Were it not for the influences of skepticism and infidelity and conscious guilt, such a tendency of thought and feeling toward the unseen and eternal world would be universal and powerful among mankind—so powerful as most materially to moderate the ardor of earthly attachments and the eagerness of earthly pursuits; for all have many friends who have crossed the mysterious gulf between time and eternity, and all are on its brink and must follow, none knows how soon, none knows how suddenly." *

It *is* most reasonable as well as exceedingly Christian to meditate on the future world, and to receive all the instruction about it that can be communicated.

"There are three things," said an old monkish chronicler, "which often make me sad: first, that I know I must die; second, that I know not when; third, that I am ignorant where I shall then be."† Even many who indulge the hope of salvation through the blood of the crucified Redeemer, and have no overruling fear of death, permit the happiness of their hope to lose some of its ecstasy by remaining content with the possession of very vague and indefinite notions as to the various elements of their eternal life; while to others who

* "The Dead in Christ," by John Brown, D.D., p. 11.

† Alge 's "Critical History of the Doctrine of a Future Life," p. 6.

have comparatively clear views of heaven after the resurrection, the condition of the soul between death and that event is one of great darkness. Some melancholy verses of a German poet, it is feared, express the feelings of not a few believers in the Bible:

"By the shore of time, now lying
On the inky flood beneath,
Patiently, thou soul undying,
Waits for thee the ship of death.

"He who on that vessel starteth,
Sailing from the sons of men,
To the friends from whom he parteth
Never more returns again.

"From her mast no flag is flying
To denote from whence she came;
She is known unto the dying,
Azael is her captain's name.

"Not a word was ever spoken
On that dark unfathomed sea;
Silence there is so unbroken
She herself seems not to be.

"Silent thus in darkness lonely
Does the soul put forth alone,
While the wings of angels only
Waft her to a land unknown."

Gloomy and forbidding the prospect! It would have been enough to chill the soul of Jesus himself. But the land which stretches up from the silvery thread of the Jordan is not an unknown land. It is not a region of silence unbroken; it is vocal with songs of praise to God. The soul does not in darkness lonely put forth into it alone, for the natural sun has scarcely ceased to enlighten the eye of the body ere the sunrise of glory beams on the released spirit. The land to which it goes is far away from earth, but it is entered by the dying believer with a more than telegraphic rapidity. The space between the Old World and the New is now annihilated by the submarine cable; Christ long ago brought into direct communion the land of glory and the land of sin. Although none of our friends, who have gone before us, return to tell about their happy home,—as the emigrant sometimes goes back to the scene of his boyhood in Ireland or Germany to report to his relatives and acquaintances the richness of this land beyond the flood, or as the spies returned from Canaan to the wilderness bearing with them the clusters of Eshcol as an earnest for the Israelites of what a rich place the land of promise was,—our great Redeemer came directly from heaven and returned to it, and has told us much about it.

On a subject which so far transcends human experience we need to speak with caution. It is dangerous to speculate upon it. We recognize here no other authority than the word of God. It is only what he has directly declared, or what may be fairly inferred from his plain declarations, that we desire decidedly to exhibit. As Dr. Owen long ago said: "When God does not speak on such topics, it is our wisdom to be silent. If the light of his truth does not go before us, we had better stand still." But God has said more about this than many suppose, and we seek, as far as possible, to draw from his word what he has revealed and to exhibit it in this little book. We cannot adopt the words of a recent rationalistic author: "The majestic theme of our immortality allures yet baffles us. No fleshly implements of logic or cunning tact of brain can reach to the solution. That secret lies in a tissueless realm whereof no nerve can report beforehand. We must wait a little. Soon we shall grope and guess no more, but grasp and know."* We do not wish to grope or guess at all; we only desire to read what God has revealed. Messages have come to us from the unseen world. They tell us something about it—very little, doubtless, in comparison with what we shall see hereafter. We know only in part. The reality will be infinitely more glorious than we can now imagine. But the descriptions that are given, as far as they go, are certain; and they are fitted to cheer us while we are here, and to make

* Alger's "Critical History of the Doctrine of a Future Life," p. 6.

us yearn for the full realization in the hereafter.

The germ of the whole Bible truth on the subject will be found in the Saviour's assurance to the dying penitent: "To-day shalt thou be with me in paradise." Luke xxiii. 43. That gives the name of the abode of the blessed souls; teaches the immediateness of their entrance to it; and involves their condition in it.

We shall exhibit—

I. Paradise,—the word, its meaning and history;

II. The inhabitants of paradise;

III. The locality in the universe of paradise;

IV. The state of saved souls in paradise;

V. The employment of souls in paradise;

VI. The holiness and happiness of souls and their mansions in paradise.

Our object is predominantly practical and comforting, though at times, and especially in the beginning, we must be historical and exegetical in order that we may exhibit the broad and deep foundation on which the practical truths are based. We also aim to neutralize some errors that are in vogue and somewhat fascinating for sentimental and uninstructed minds; but we seek to do this, not in a controversial way, by a reference to the errors and a formal refutation of them, but by the direct and positive exhibition of the revelations which they deny or distort.

Keeping in mind this practical character of the book, we shall not burden its pages by the statements of conflicting opinions that have been advanced on different points, or by lengthy references to authorities that have been consulted.

It is only necessary to add that the view which we aim to elaborate and popularize is the one which is presented in the thirty-third chapter of the "Westminster Confession of Faith:"

"The bodies of men, after death, return

to dust and see corruption ; but their souls (which neither die nor sleep), having an immortal subsistence, immediately return to God who gave them. The souls of the righteous, being then made perfect in holiness, are received into the highest heavens, where they behold the face of God in light and glory, waiting for the full redemption of their bodies ; and the souls of the wicked are cast into hell, where they remain in torments and utter darkness, reserved to the judgment of the great day. Besides these two places for souls separated from their bodies, the Scripture acknowledgeth none."

CHAPTER II.

PARADISE.—THE WORD AND THE PLACE.

THE word paradise is probably of Persian origin. Thence it came to us through the Greek language, in which it was first naturalized by Xenophon, "who designated by it the parks or pleasure-gardens of Persia." In the Greek translation of the Old Testament called the Septuagint, which was made in the third century before Christ, it was used to express any stately garden of delight. But pre-eminently it designated the garden in Eden which was the original residence of our first parents: "The Lord God planted *a paradise* eastward in Eden." Thus it has come to us, so that, though it does not appear either in the Hebrew of the Old Tesment or in our English translation of it, it is the name which we almost universally apply to the birth-home of our race. The ideas associated with it are beauty and exquisite delight; and the word, being a metaphor for those ideas, appears in New Testament times in a higher application, for the clear understanding of which it will be necessary to go back and bring together two diverse trains of thought.

The Old Testament revelations of the future worlds have not the clearness and the fullness of the New Testament; it remained for Jesus Christ to bring life and immortality to light through the gospel. All through the sacred books, however, the distinction between soul and body and the union in man of the two natures are taught. "The Lord God formed man of the dust of the ground, and breathed into his nostrils the breath of life; and man became a living soul." Gen. ii. 7. The royal preacher declared that at death "shall the dust return to the earth as it was, and the spirit shall return unto God who gave it." Eccles. xii. 7. Moses twice addressed the Lord as "the God of the spirits of all flesh." Num. xvi. 22 and xxvii. 16. Such passages assume the truth which our Redeemer asserted when he said: "Fear not them which kill the body, but are not able to kill the soul; but rather fear Him which is able to destroy both soul and body in hell." Matt. x. 28.

Furthermore, the continued existence of the soul after the death of the body, the fact that it does not cease to live when the body dies—in other words, its immortality—lies at the foundation of the Jewish scriptures. The great promise of the ancient revelation, which was apprehended and trusted in by the believers in God, embodied an inheritance after death in "a better country, that is, an heavenly." Heb. xi. 16. The full-orbed sun of immortality did not appear above the horizon until Christ arose from the grave and came back from death to life, but the harbingers of his coming were over the heavens,

> "As rays around the source of light
> Stream upward ere he glow in sight,
> And watching by his future flight,
> Set the clear heavens on fire."

Our Redeemer declared that Moses taught the truth of the unbroken existence of the soul. In a conversation with the Sadducees, who denied the doctrine of the resurrection, he said: "Now that the dead are raised, even Moses showed at the bush when he calleth the Lord the God of Abraham, and the God of Isaac, and the God of Jacob. For he is not a God of the dead, but of the living: for all live unto him." Luke xx. 37, 38. This is a very explicit divine comment. It teaches that the patriarchs were still living and waiting for the resurrection of their bodies; and that as they were, so are all—immortal. The translations of Enoch and Elijah and the history of the reappearance of Samuel at Endor—explain that history as we may—kept the truth prominently before the minds of the Jews.

In portraying the future world the Spirit of inspiration, adapting the dress with which he clothed his thoughts to the development of the minds of the Jews, seized hold of sensible things to image forth the invisible. The bodies of the righteous and the wicked both died and were buried in the same manner. The same Hebrew term, *sheol*, was, therefore, applied in the Bible to the grave of each. Thus a general assertion which will include both classes is made in the prayer of Hannah: "The Lord killeth and maketh alive: he bringeth down to *sheol* and bringeth up." 1 Sam. ii. 6. David, in giving an injunction to Solomon for the punishment of a man of blood, said: "Let not his hoar head go down to *sheol* in peace." 1 Kings ii. 6. On the other hand, the righteous spake of that as the resting-place of their bodies. In his agony at the loss of Joseph, Jacob refused to be comforted, and said: "I will go down into *sheol* unto my son mourning." Gen. xxxvii. 35. Job said: "Oh that thou wouldest hide me in *sheol*, that thou wouldest keep me secret, until thy wrath be past, that thou wouldest appoint me a set time, and remember me" (Job xiv. 13); and again: "If I wait *sheol* is mine house: I have made my bed in the darkness. I have said to corruption, Thou art my father: to the worm, Thou art my mother and my sister. And where is now my hope? as for my hope who shall see it? They shall go down to the bars of the pit, when our rest together is in the dust." Job xvii. 13–16. And God, by the mouth of Hosea, uttered a promise which is full of encouragement to believers: "I will ransom them from the power of *sheol;* I will redeem them from death: O death, I will be thy plagues: O *sheol*, I will be thy destruction." Hos. xiii. 14. In none of these passages is there a reference to the place of departed spirits, either saved or lost. The declaration of Job especially shows that the temporary resting-place of the dead body is referred to.

The grave was a gloomy and forbidding place. Its associations were disagreeable. Nature shrank from it. Lonely, silent, dark, shut out from the world of life and activity, human nature desires not to go to it. Hence, assuming the continued existence of the soul, the same term easily came to be applied to the place where the departed spirits of the wicked went at death. How very close is the association in our Lord's description of the rich man: "He died, and was buried and in hell (hades) he lift up his eyes, being in torment." Luke xvi. 23. The force of that expression can almost be felt. The dying and dropping of the body into the grave was the dropping of the soul into hell. In Psalm ix. 17 it is declared that "the wicked shall be turned into *sheol*." In the fourteenth chapter of Isaiah, in language of fearful imagery, the wicked king of Babylon is represented as entering this place and being received with taunting exultation by those who had preceded him.

Thus not only the bodies, but the souls, of the wicked go to a gloomy region. This is pictured to us as under ground, in the lower parts of the earth, as far as possible from heaven—the very opposite of heaven, indeed. Thus: "It is as high as heaven; what canst thou do? Deeper than *sheol;* what canst thou know?" Job xi. 8. "Though they dig into *sheol,* thence shall my hand take them; though they climb up to heaven, thence will I bring them down." Amos ix. 2. "A fire is kindled in mine anger, and hath burned unto the lowest *sheol,* and hath consumed the earth with her increase, and set on fire the foundations of the mountains." Deut. xxxii. 22. "If I ascend up into heaven, thou art there; if I make my bed in *sheol,* behold, thou art there." Ps. cxxxix. 8. The same name is given to the place of the dead body and to the place of the lost soul, the former just below the earth, or in a recess excavated out of the earth, the latter far beneath and far away from heaven, but both very gloomy and repulsive places.

Nowhere, however, in the Old Testament did the Holy Spirit teach that the spirits of the just went to any such place on the death of their bodies.* Their bodies

* Passages in which it might seem, at first sight, that Old Testament saints spake of their souls going to *sheol* as an intermediate place between earth and heaven may, we think, be explained by the fact that the two natures, the physical and the spiritual, are so united in the one person of a man that what is true only of the body is habitually predicated of him. This is a common usage in every-day conversation. We say that a friend has died; we only mean that his body has died. The usage also prevailed in Bible times; and very easy and naturally the righteous dead would be so spoken of as to make it appear to a superficial reader, without the recollection of this principle, that the soul as well as the body passed into the gloomy under-ground place. Even now, with the gospel through which life and immortality are so clearly brought to light, we speak of burying a dead person, when all that we bury, and all that we intend to say we bury, is his body. The same mode of interpretation which finds in some Old Testament expressions the idea that redeemed souls went, for a season at least, to some other place than heaven, would draw from our expressions the dogma that they are hidden in the grave.

were buried in the grave—the same kind of a grave as that in which the bodies of the wicked were buried. The dust of the two mingled together. But the liberated spirits of the redeemed escaped the place of the wicked, and were received into the presence of God.

Thus the pious man of God declared: "God will redeem my soul from the power of *sheol;* for he shall receive me." Ps. xlix. 15. "For thou hast delivered my soul from death: wilt not thou deliver my feet from falling, that I may walk before God in the light of the living?" Ps. lvi. 13. "Thou hast delivered my soul from death, mine eyes from tears, and my feet from falling." Ps. cxvi. 8. "Nevertheless I am continually with thee: thou hast holden me by my right hand. Thou shalt guide me with thy counsel, and afterward receive me to glory. Whom have I in heaven but thee? and there is none upon earth that I desire beside thee. My flesh and my heart faileth:

but God is the strength of my heart and my portion for ever." Ps. lxxiii. 23–26. The prophet Isaiah asserted: "The righteous perisheth, and no man layeth it to heart: and merciful men are taken away, none considering that the righteous is taken away from the evil. He shall enter into peace: they shall rest in their beds, each one walking in his uprightness." Isa. lvii. 1. Thus, while the bodies of the righteous were lying in the bed of the grave, their souls were living in uprightness and in peace. The Messiah was prophetically represented as saying: "Thou wilt not leave my soul in *sheol* (or abandon my soul to *sheol*), neither wilt thou suffer thine holy one to see corruption." Ps. xvi. 10. That is, as the body of Jesus was not to remain long enough in the grave to become corrupt, neither was his soul to be permitted by God to go at all to the place of departed wicked spirits; it was not to be abandoned to that place.*

* Dr. J. Addison Alexander translates the passage: "Thou wilt

This is briefly the sum of the Old Testament teaching in reference to the future

not leave my soul *to* hell; thou wilt not give thy holy One to see corruption." And he adds upon it that the Psalmist "does not say *leave in*, but *to*—*i. e.*, abandon to, give up to the dominion or possession of another." Then on the second clause he says: "*Give*—*i. e.*, permit, or, more emphatically, give up, abandon, which makes the parallelism of the clauses more exact." In his comment on Acts ii. 27, where Peter quotes the Psalmist for the purpose of showing that his words referred to Jesus, Dr. Alexander further says: "*Hell*, in its old and wide sense of the unseen world (hades), the world of spirits, the state of the soul separated from the body without any reference to happiness or misery. The essential meaning is, Thou wilt not leave my soul and body separate." Dr. Fairbairn, however, in his *Hermeneutical Manual* (Section, "Import and Use of Hades in Scripture"), while through a failure to discriminate between the soul and the body in the Old Testament passages where *sheol* is used, he admits that the place was regarded as the abode after death alike of the good and the bad, yet, speaking of *hades* (which, as will be seen further on, is the Greek translation of *sheol*), remarks that "it cannot but be regarded as a noticeable circumstance that in the solitary example wherein *hades* is mentioned by our Lord explicitly as a receptacle of the departed, it is in connection with the wicked and as a place of torment." p. 324. He alludes further to "the studied avoidance on the part of our Lord of the term *hades* to denote the place of his temporary sojourn and that of his people between death and the resurrection." p. 325. Then, rebutting the notion of "the great body of Christian writers" places. The bodies and souls of the wicked went to gloomy and repulsive abodes. The

who hold that the passage in Acts is "conclusive as to the fact of Christ's soul having actually been in *hades*, since it could not have been represented as not left there had it not actually been there," and mentioning that "by many of them it is deemed the only very clear and decisive text on the point," he says: "The words in the Greek which represent quite exactly the sense of the Hebrew are, Thou wilt not relinquish, or abandon, my soul to hades—wilt not surrender it as a helpless prey to that hostile power or unwelcome abode. It might, indeed, mean that the soul was to be allowed to enter there, though not to be shut up for a continuance, but it might also, and *even more naturally*, intimate that the soul should not properly fall under the dominion of hades." pp. 325, 326. This, which is the more natural interpretation of the words, seems to us, in the light of the general teaching of the Bible, to be the real one. It is greatly to be regretted that we circulate the so-called Apostles' Creed with the clause that Christ "descended into hell," especially in view of the restricted meaning which the word "hell" now has. Some of the early fathers, in their citation of the creed, omit the clause. Even such writers as Irenæus and Tertullian, in their summaries of the Christian faith, have nothing like it. The popular mind understands it as teaching what is a most serious error. To this the gentle Archbishop Leighton refers almost contemptuously in his Exposition of the Creed: "*Descended into hell.* The more noise there hath been about this clause, I shall make the less. The conceit of the descent of Christ's soul into the place of the damned, to say no more nor harder of it, can never be made the bodies of the righteous were buried in the dark and repelling grave, but their spirits flew away to God.

But in order to understand a very serious departure from this which prevailed among the Jews at the coming of Christ, and to appreciate properly the teaching of the New Testament in reference to the future worlds, we must turn to a heathen opinion on the subject.

"Heathenism is man's development of

necessary sense of these words, nor is there any other ground in Scripture or any due end of such a descent, either agreed on, or at all allegeable, to persuade the choosing of it as the best sense of them. Not to contest other interpretations, I conceive with submission that it differs not much, possibly nothing, from the plain word of his burial. Not that the author or authors of this so brief a confession would express one thing by divers words, but that it may be in the more ancient copies only the one of them hath been in the text, and in after copies in transcriber's hands the other hath crept into it out of the margin. But retaining it by all means as it is, it may signify the abode and continuance of Christ's body in the grave, in which time he seemed to have been swallowed up of death, and that the pit had shut her mouth on him; but it appeared quickly otherwise, for *the third* day he arose from the dead." (See pp. 44 and 72, *notes*.)

God's revelation, and is related to the ancient dispensation as Romanism to the Christian."* The early heathen families and nations wandered off from those who had the knowledge of the true God by direct communication, and in their wanderings carried with them portions of the truth which they had received in the cradle of the race; but being left to themselves, without God in the world, they sooner or later entirely forgot, or greatly perverted and corrupted, the portion that they had taken with them. Japhet and Ham, as well as Shem, received the instructions of their father Noah. Ishmael, as well as Isaac, the child of the covenant, was taught by Abraham. And the descendants of Ishmael and of Japhet and Ham, even after their departure from God, retained something of their early instructions, as one who is stolen away from his home in boyhood will keep in his mind through all the vicious training that he may receive

* "Princeton Review," xxxvii. 349.

some of the lessons which he learned from his mother; though, being left without continued revelations and without a written volume in which the truth was preserved infallibly, what they had learned became dimmer and more and more mixed with error. This accounts for the fact that among heathen nations vague traditions of the great scriptural events are still found. Thousands of years of sin and darkness have not entirely destroyed the memory of the creation, the fall and the flood. This is also one of the incidental proofs that God has made of one blood all nations of men to dwell on all the face of the earth. They have this common heritage.

This truth of the continued existence of the soul after death is one which has always prevailed among mankind. In all nations a deep-seated conviction of it prevailed as a part of the popular creed before it received any scientific form from philosophers. The Greeks, with whom we have specially to deal here, held that there was a place called *hades*. It was under ground, lower than the earth. The souls of all the dead were carried to it. It contained two divisions; one was Elysium, the abode of the good, the other was Tartarus, the abode of the bad. The predominant notion of the whole place in both of its divisions, however, was gloomy and forbidding. Existence there was shadowy; it was something between life and death. The passage to it from the life of earth was a change from light to darkness. So undesirable was it that in Hades the Achilles of Homer declared he would rather till a field on earth as a day-laborer than rule all the hosts of the shades.

The Jews in their dispersion met with this opinion. Many of them had settled in Egypt, which had come under Greek influence. Their Hebrew language had become almost a dead tongue, and for their use a translation of their Scriptures into the Greek, which was then the fashionable cosmopolitan language of the world of scholars, was made nearly three hundred years before Christ. This is what is called the Septuagint. It was very much in use in the time of our Saviour. The apostle Paul, being a learned Grecian, frequently quoted from it in his Epistles instead of from the Hebrew. It has had an important influence on the Christian Church.

In that version of the Old Testament the word *hades* was used as the translation of the *sheol* which in the Hebrew Scriptures designated the place of dead bodies and the place of wicked disembodied spirits. In the later period of the Jewish commonwealth the two words were viewed as substantially of the same import. Very naturally, as the Jews became perverted by the philosophy of the heathen, the heathen notion was attached by them to the scriptural name. Hence they came to look upon their *sheol* as an immense place where good and bad spirits both existed in a separate state between the death and the resurrection of their bodies. The resurrection was a notion which the heathen had not. In this the greater part of the Jews continued to differ from them. The heathen regarded their *hades* as the final place; the Jews thought of it as an intermediate one. Josephus, the Jewish historian, who lived shortly after our Redeemer, thus describes the belief of the Pharisees: "They believe that souls have an immortal vigor in them, and that under the earth there will be rewards or punishments, according as they have lived virtuously or viciously in this life; that the latter are to be detained in everlasting prison, but that the former shall have power to revive and live again."* It is contended by some, however, that, while the Pharisees used the word resurrection, all that they intended by it was the existence of the soul and its transmigration into other bodies; for it would seem that many of them had adopted the notion

* "Antiquities of the Jews," xviii. 1, 3.

of the passage of the spirit from one body to another—not merely another human body, but even that of a brute—on account of sin committed in its previous body, and as a means of purification. Hence the question which was put to our Lord in reference to the man who was blind from his birth: "Who did sin, this man or his parents, that he was born blind?" John ix. 2. This explanation, held in connection with the fact that Jesus answered men according to their meaning, will show that when he replied, "Neither hath this man sinned nor his parents" (John ix. 3), he meant to deny not original or actual sin, but that absurd mode in which the errorists held sin was dealt with. It was under the influence of the same error that the Messiah was looked upon as Elijah, or Jeremiah, or one of the prophets, in a new body. So, too, in the apocryphal book of Wisdom, written under the taint of the Grecian philosophy, the idea was expressed in these words: "I was a witty child, and had a good spirit; yea, rather being good I came into a body undefiled."

The Jews, who through contact with the heathen philosophy had deviated from the faith of their fathers, supposed the region of the blessed to be in the upper part of this *hades*, or the invisible and intermediate place of disembodied souls, but still below the earth and away from heaven; while under it was the abyss or *gehenna* in which the souls of the wicked were subjected to punishment. To the former they gave the name of *Paradise*.

It can easily be understood how the ideal beauty of the dwelling-place of our first parents, perhaps also the fact that it had vanished from the earth, caused its name to be transferred to that region and province in *hades*, or the invisible world, where the souls of the faithful were supposed to be gathered waiting for the perfect consummation and bliss. "As paradise, or the garden of Eden, was a place of great beauty, pleasure and tranquillity, so the state of separate souls was a state of peace and excellent delight."* It was supposed to be "a far-off land, a region where there was no scorching heat, no consuming cold, where the soft west wind from the ocean blew for evermore." "There was no night there. The pavement of the place was of precious stones. Plants of healing power and wonderful fragrance grew on the banks of its streams. Streams of milk and honey were there, along which were twelve trees laden with divers fruits, and mighty mountains reared their heads, whereon grew lilies and roses. As the righteous dead entered it angels stripped them of their grave-clothes, arrayed them in robes of glory, and placed on their heads diadems of gold and pearls."†

The word thus in use was taken by our Redeemer and applied to the abode of the

* Trench's "Epistles to the Seven Churches," p. 128.

† Smith's Dictionary of the Bible, art. *Paradise.*

blessed beyond the grave, though it is worthy of note that it occurs only three times in our Bible, the place being described in other ways which reveal more fully its glories. And *Hades*, with Gehenna and Tartarus, is confined in the New Testament to that region of the future world which is under the power of the evil one, and where the wicked are suffering for their sins. If *hades*, as it is used in the New Testament, meant the general receptacle of disembodied spirits, it would make that portion of the divine volume teach that the souls of the just are in some way under Satan until the judgment; which is against the general and explicit declarations of the Scriptures. In the only sentence where Jesus himself uses the word for the place of departed souls, it designates the region of torment. That is in the parable of the rich man and Lazarus: "The rich man also died and was buried; and in hell (*hades*) he lift up his eyes, being in torments." Luke xvi. 23. The assertion that "he seeth Abraham afar off" intimates that the two were not in two apartments of the same place. Moreover, between the two places there is a great impassable gulf.

But while the sacred writers use the word paradise to designate the place of the blessed, they purify it from its erroneous meaning. It was too precious a name to be abandoned to error. Its associations for the human race were too delightful to be permitted to cluster around any place near the abode of the lost. It is not used in the New Testament, therefore, to designate an intermediate place just below the earth and forming one apartment of an abode distinct from heaven, the other apartment of which the doomed inhabit. Ah, no! redeemed souls pass through no such place to reach the presence of their Lord. While the word retains every good meaning that the Jews had given it, it is purified from its baser elements, as the Spirit of inspiration purifies every human word that he adopts, and is carried up to heaven itself; for the paradise of the blessed is heaven.

The apostle Paul says in 2 Cor. xii. 1–4: "It is not expedient for me doubtless to glory. I will come to visions and revelations of the Lord. I knew a man in Christ above fourteen years ago (whether in the body, I cannot tell; or whether out of the body, I cannot tell: God knoweth); such an one caught up to the third heaven. And I knew such a man (whether in the body, or out of the body, I cannot tell: God knoweth); how that he was caught up into paradise, and heard unspeakable words, which it is not lawful for a man to utter." It is admitted that the apostle here speaks of himself. He is referring to a vision that he had seen. So great was the effect which it had produced on him, so exalted was his ecstasy, that he could not tell whether his soul had been for a time taken out of the body and carried aloft, or whether body and soul both had been caught up to the blessed place. It made him also allude to the vision twice. That he refers to only one vision is evident. The time of the two references is the same. If they were to be interpreted as describing two separate visions, it would follow that paradise was even a more exalted and ravishing place than the third heaven, because it is in the verse which mentions paradise that the apostle declares he heard words which it is not lawful or possible for man to utter. But this repetition of the vision is caused by that impetuosity of style which marks the writings of Paul. Perhaps, too, he intended directly to combat the perverted Jewish notion, as if he had said: I call this place, first, the third heaven, the highest heaven, and I call it paradise also, to guard against the notion that paradise is a place separate from heaven, and therefore I throw out my most rapturous terms when I use that word. The third heaven and the paradise to which I was taken up are the same.

In Rev. ii. 7 our exalted Lord promises: "To him that overcometh will I give to eat of the tree of life which is in the midst of the paradise of God." Turn over to the first two verses of the twenty-second chapter: "And he showed me a pure river of water of life clear as crystal, proceeding out of the throne of God and of the Lamb. In the midst of the street of it, and on either side of the river, was there the tree of life which bare twelve manner of fruits, and yielded her fruit every month: and the leaves of the tree were for the healing of the nations." That is a description of heaven—no intermediate place below the earth, but the place where the throne of God and the Lamb is, the place of perfect happiness, the vision of which is enough to thrill the soul and almost translate it ere the trammels of the body are laid aside. But the tree of life, which in the beginning of the book appears in paradise, is there: so that paradise and heaven, the place of God's throne, are the same.

The apostle Paul declares in 2 Cor. v. 6–8 that "whilst we are at home in the body, we are absent from the Lord (for we walk by faith, not by sight): we are confident, I say, and willing rather to be absent from the body, and to be present with the Lord." That ought to settle beyond all cavil the place of saved souls immediately after death. Between death and the resurrection they are absent from the body and present with the Lord. Wherever he is in his glorified form they are.

If we need any further corroboration of this, it is found in Eph. iii. 15, where it is declared that "of our Lord Jesus Christ the whole family in heaven and earth is named." All the members of the redeemed family of God are either in heaven or on earth. There is no intermediate place that holds any of them. The only other place is the abode of the lost, and into that no believing penitent soul sinks for an instant; from it no soul ever reaches heaven, for between the two there is a great gulf fixed, and they that would pass from one to the other cannot.

The idea of an intermediate place—whether it take the form of a *limbus patrum*, where Old Testament believers remained without the beatific vision of God, yet without suffering, until the death of Christ; or of a *limbus infantum*, where the souls of unbaptized infants go, and where they enjoy not the vision of God, though they endure no positive suffering; or of purgatory, where partially sanctified Christians are purified through sufferings in material fire; or of a region where the disembodied souls of the good and bad both await the resurrection of their bodies before going to God or to Satan—is essentially of heathen origin. Our earth, in its existing form, hell and heaven are the only three places for the present abode of human spirits which the Bible reveals to us; and from the body the soul is taken either to heaven or hell without passing into an intermediate place of any kind.

The soul of Jesus went immediately from the cross to paradise:* "Father, into thy hands I commend my spirit." Luke xxiii.

* The contradictions into which those fall who reject this view are striking. Thus Olshausen, adopting the doctrine that man consists of three distinct substances, body, soul and spirit, and feeling the force of the Redeemer's words, holds that at his death his spirit returned to the Father. But Stier, acknowledging also the force of those words, but having accepted the erroneous idea of Paradise, says ("Words of the Lord Jesus," iii. 695), "Nevertheless, Christ's spirit did not at once go up to heaven (the word to the malefactor would contradict this), thither where the eternal Son was before; that did not take place until the glorified flesh could go there too." And he thus in a note quotes Olshausen: "While the *soul* of Christ went to the dead in sheol (but 1 Pet. iii. 18 testifies against that) and his body rested in the sepulchre, his spirit returned to the Father. In the resurrection all was reunited into a harmonious unity."

Our risen Lord's words to Mary Magdalene are sometimes cited against our view. The Rev. Edward Henry Bickersteth's "Yesterday, To-day and For Ever" is a poem of rare beauty and much delightful truth, notwithstanding its grave underlying error of an intermediate place. It was reviewed and its error in this particular exposed by the writer of this book in an article

46. The soul of the pardoned malefactor dying at his side ascended at the same time to the same place: "*To-day* shalt thou be *with me* in paradise." In his glorified body Jesus returned again to the glorious region

in *The Presbyterian*, of Philadelphia, of January 16, 1869. Mr. Bickersteth replied to that article in a letter, which was published with a rejoinder to it, March 20, 1869. In that letter he wrote: "When you say, 'We prefer to think that the Lord is now in the very heaven of heavens,' I heartily agree with you—I think so too; but when you immediately proceed to say, 'The soul of Jesus went directly there—*i. e.*, to the very heaven of heavens —from the cross, and returned again to his body the third day,' I must entirely dissent from your views. If this were so, how could he have said to Mary Magdalene in the garden after his resurrection: 'Touch me not, for I am not yet ascended to my Father'?" John xx. 17. But manifestly that declaration of the Saviour meant that he had not yet ascended *in the body*. *Touch me not.* It does not imply that his *soul* had not gone there from the cross. Similar to this is the declaration of Peter after our Lord's bodily ascension, that "David is not yet ascended into the heavens." The passage refers to the resurrection and place of the body, and not to the soul. The bodily ascension David was and is yet to experience. The well-understood doctrine of the κοινωνία ἰδιωματων flowing from the union of the two distinct substances soul and body in the one person of man (see Hodge's "Systematic Theology," ii. 379) explains all such declarations. A person may affirm of himself an act which belongs only to his body. (See pp. 25 and 72, *notes.*)

forty days after his resurrection, and there he has ever since abode.

How significant of the beauty of the place, of ever-present communion with God, of perfect holiness and pure happiness, is this title of heaven! Recognizing the promise made to the penitent malefactor as the heritage of all believing souls, into the enjoyment of which they enter immediately on the death of the body, how enrapturing the prospect for us!

It has already been intimated that the heathen nations have not entirely forgotten the great facts of the early sacred history, though, as the result of their wandering off from God's revelation into the wilderness of sin, they hold them in very perverted forms. The remembrance of an earthly paradise is a part of the common heritage of the race. In Hindoo literature, next to the sacred books perhaps the most ancient literature of the world, "man is presented as the creature of God, as capable of righteousness, but as having sinned and forfeited the favor of God thereby." "In the centre of Jambu-dwipa, the middle of the seven continents of the Purânas, is the golden mountain Meru, which stands like the seed-cup of the lotus of the earth. On its summit is the vast city of Brahma, renowned in heaven and encircled by the Ganges, which, issuing from the foot of the Vishnu, washes the lunar orb, and falling thither from the skies, is divided into four streams that flow to the four corners of the earth. In this abode of divinity is the Naudana, or grove of Indra; there, too, is the Jambu tree, from whose fruit are fed the waters of the Jambu river, which give life and immortality to all who drink thereof."

"Arab legends tell of a garden in the East, on the summit of a mountain of jacinth, inaccessible to man—a garden of rich soil and equable temperature, well watered and abounding with trees and flowers of rare colors and fragrance."

In the Græco-Roman literature, with which we are most acquainted through the authors that are a part of the educational training of boys in our classical schools, comparatively rationalistic and infidel as that period was, we meet with a golden age of innocence and happiness. "Truth and right prevailed, though not enforced by law, nor was there any majesty to threaten and punish. The forest had not yet been robbed of its trees to furnish timber for vessels, nor had men built fortifications around their towns. There were no such things as swords, spears or helmets. The earth brought forth all things necessary for man without his labor in ploughing or sowing. Perpetual spring reigned, flowers sprang up without seed, the rivers flowed with milk and wine, and yellow honey distilled from the oaks."

"All these and similar traditions are but mere mocking echoes of the old Hebrew story, jarred and broken notes of the same strain; but with all their exaggerations, they intimate how in the background of man's visions lay a paradise of holy joy; a paradise secured from every kind of profanation and made inaccessible to the guilty; a paradise full of objects that were calculated to delight the senses and to elevate the mind; a paradise that granted to its tenant rich and rare immunities, and that fed with its perennial streams the tree of life and immortality."

In the history of the heathen, as they wandered off from the light, fable and speculation thus became mixed with the truths which we believe on the authority of the sacred word. Its facts are grandly simple. When God had created man, he placed him in a garden which was the beautiful abode of holiness and happiness. After the race had sinned it was cast forth from that garden, and paradise itself was removed from earth. It was committed to the charge of cherubim, and a flaming sword at its gate turned every way to keep the way of the tree of life. Paradise was lost; but the words uttered by the Redeemer on the cross of his satisfaction to God for our sins tell us of a paradise restored. They proclaim his lordship over it and the admission into it of every soul saved by him. What Adam lost through the subtilty of the evil one, our Redeemer by his sacrificial death regained. Above earth's waste wilderness, cursed for sin and bringing forth thorns and thistles, the garden of Eden is raised again. Adam took out of paradise all his descendants because they were in him and involved in his sin. Christ takes back to paradise all who are in him under the gracious covenant, and who, therefore, receive his righteousness. And as it is the prerogative of Christ and his gospel not only to overcome and banish sin, but to ennoble, to elevate, to multiply every good thing that they touch, the paradise that *is* far excels the paradise that *was*:

"Though that seat of earthly bliss be failed,
A fairer paradise is founded now
For Adam and his chosen sons."

The light of a gorgeous beauty rests upon it such as the primeval garden was never bathed in. Its colors appear the richer because the grace of God has painted them on the black clouds of sin, as the sun shows his most beautiful tints in the rainbow upon the watery clouds. It is *the* place of creation. It has

"An ampler ether, a diviner air,
And fields invested with purpureal gleams,
Climes which the Sun who sheds the brightest day
Earth owns is all unworthy to survey."

It has the highest spiritual beauty; no sin is in it, and therefore tears of sorrow never fall therein; it is never broken up into the graves of lost hopes; its atmosphere is never ruffled with the voice of crying or the exclamation of pain. Through it, as it is pictured on the inspired pages, runs a river whose waters never overflow to destroy, and whose clear crystal bosom, undisturbed by storms, brightly reflects the ever-shining glory of God. Streets of a golden brilliancy that never dims lead up through it from gates that have all the purity of pearls — highways of glory and of excellency over which no curse is scattered, and which are not deformed by the thorns and weeds of a sin-bearing soil. Joy and gladness are found therein, thanksgiving and the voice of melody from the innumerable multitude of the ransomed who sing the song of glory to the Lamb. In the centre is a throne with a rainbow round about it in sight like unto an emerald, upon which, in the land of beauty the most beautiful of all, is the gracious and glorious One whose promise thrills our heart with the ecstatic hope of the place. It would not be paradise without him; his presence makes it; and there he is. The veil between it and us is now so thin that, in the gorgeous visions of the beloved disciple, we can almost see through it and behold him. He is the same that he was on earth, but how different in appearance! He is glorified now. He wears a body which is too bright for the gaze of the unglorified eye, for it made the apostle in his apocalyptic vision fall down as dead. No longer on the cross, but on the throne! No longer the despised of earth, with only a dying thief to confess him, but a King reigning over the universe, the cynosure of all eyes, the judge of all creatures! His head and his hairs are white like wool, as white as snow; his eyes are as a flame of fire; his feet like unto fine brass, as if they burned in a furnace; and his voice as the sound of many waters. He has in his right hand seven stars; out of his mouth goes a sharp two-edged sword; and his countenance is as the sun shineth in his strength; and he declares, "I am the first and the last: I am he that liveth and was dead; and behold I am alive for evermore; and have the keys of hades and of death." Rev. i. 12–18.

CHAPTER III.

THE INHABITANTS OF PARADISE.

YE are come unto Mount Zion, and unto the city of the living God, the heavenly Jerusalem, and to an innumerable company of angels, to the general assembly and church of the first born, which are written in heaven, and to God the judge of all, and to the spirits of just men made perfect, and to Jesus the mediator of the new covenant, and to the blood of sprinkling that speaketh better things than that of Abel." Heb. xii. 22–24.

A grander and more soul-stirring truth than the foregoing passage contains can scarcely be found even in the word of God. By Mount Zion, the city of the living God, the heavenly Jerusalem, the apostle means heaven itself. His assertion is that believers who are still living on the earth *have come*—not are yet to come, but have actually come—unto it. The gospel dispensation, which is often called the kingdom either of God or of heaven, is viewed as "extending through time into eternity, and embracing saints on earth and angels and saints in heaven in one common family under one common head. Becoming members of Christ's Church, we are united to that blessed family whose home and seat are in heaven." *

The Church of God is one. Its members who have left the earth have ascended to the metropolitan city of their kingdom—a city which is daily enlarging, and which is to extend until it shall include the innumerable multitude of Christ's redeemed. Those who are still on the earth are citizens of the same city, living now in a far-off part of the land indeed, but destined to go

* Sampson's Commentary on Hebrews, *in loc.*

up also to the capital. They who have entered never more go out. We who are still in the borders of the kingdom are traveling toward it, and shall finally sit down there with Abraham and Isaac and Jacob, with the prophets, the apostles and the martyrs, with the saved of all ages, and with our own departed friends in Christ. Precious truth to them and to us, because in the one kingdom we have an interest in the one city; our citizenship is there.

"One family we dwell in him,
One Church above, beneath,
Though now divided by the stream,
The narrow stream, of death.

"One army of the living God,
To his commands we bow;
Part of the host have crossed the flood,
And part are crossing now."

This designation of heaven as a city is by no means rare. Both the place itself and its redeemed inhabitants, because of their everlasting and intimate connection with it, are thus exhibited over and over again: "Abraham looked for a city which hath foundations, whose builder and maker is God." Heb. xi. 10. "These all died in faith, not having received the promises, but having seen them afar off, and were persuaded of them and embraced them, and confessed that they were strangers and pilgrims on the earth. For they that say such things declare plainly that they seek a country. And truly, if they had been mindful of that country from whence they came out, they might have had opportunity to have returned. But now they desire a better country, that is an heavenly: wherefore God is not ashamed to be called their God, for he hath prepared for them a city." Heb. xi. 13–16. "Here we have no continuing city, but we seek one to come." Heb. xiii. 14. "This Agar is Mount Sinai in Arabia, and answereth to the Jerusalem which now is, and is in bondage with her children. But Jerusalem which is above is free, which is the mother of us all." Gal. iv. 25, 26. "Him that overcometh will I make a pillar in the temple of my God, and he shall go no more out: and I will write upon him the name of my God, and the name of the city of my God, which is new Jerusalem, which cometh down out of heaven from my God." Rev. iii. 12. "I John saw the holy city, new Jerusalem, coming down from God out of heaven, prepared as a bride adorned for her husband. . . . And he carried me away in the spirit to a great and high mountain, and showed me that great city, the holy Jerusalem, descending out of heaven from God, having the glory of God." Rev. xxi. 2, 10. "Blessed are they that do his commandments, that they may have right to the tree of life, and may enter in through the gates into the city." Rev. xxii. 14.

An explanation of the way in which Jerusalem thus became a type of heaven and gave its name to the blessed place will in a very beautiful manner show the connection of the topic of this chapter with the history which we have given of the word paradise—a connection intimated in the last verse that has just been quoted—and it will form an additional and winning picture of the abode of glorified souls.

On the expulsion of our first parents from the garden of Eden, God placed at the east of it cherubim and a flaming sword which turned every way to keep the way of the tree of life. The cherubim reappear in various subsequent passages of the Bible. By Ezekiel and by John they are called living creatures. (It is an unhappy thing that in Revelation, chapters iv.–vi., the word is translated "beasts.") They are always represented to be in the place where God in a peculiar manner manifests his glory,—as in the most holy place of the tabernacle, in the oracle of the temple, bearing up the throne of God while (in the visions of Ezekiel) it hastens forward to execute the decrees of justice, and then, finally, at the great consummation of all things, before that throne of God's awful majesty from which, in the apocalyptic vision, proceeded lightnings and thunderings and voices. Ex. xxv. 18; 1 Kings vi. 23; Heb. ix. 5; Ezek. x. 5; Rev. iv., v., vi. John saw them in a posture of reverence and adoration before God. With the four and twenty elders "they fell down before the Lamb, having every one of them harps, and golden vials full of odors which are the prayers of the saints. And they sang a new song, saying, Thou art worthy to take the book and to open the seals thereof: for thou wast slain, and hast redeemed us to God by thy blood out of every kindred and tongue and people and nation; and hast made us unto our God kings and priests: and we shall reign on the earth." Rev. v. 8–10. The living creatures in heaven, then, represent redeemed men; and the placing of the figures in the garden of Eden had this meaning: For his sin man has been banished from the happy place. He has failed to keep that which was committed to him. He is shut out from the tree of life. The flaming sword turns every way, a type of the everywhere-looking and everywhere-present holiness and justice of God, which would cut down and destroy the sinner. But mercy is mingled with justice. Already has God given intimations of redemption; for the great enemy who had tempted man is to be overthrown by a descendant of the tempted pair. While the flaming sword turns, with it there are the cherubim to show that the way of the tree of life shall still be kept. Notwithstanding man's suicidal failure, God has not for ever banished him; the cherubim are in the garden a type of man redeemed and glorified entering the heavenly paradise, and receiving from Him who has the power over it, and who himself in human form overcame the great enemy, the right to the tree of life. In paradise lost, and wherever else they appeared, the cherubim told of paradise to be restored

Thus we bring together the beginning and the end of the Bible—the fall of man and his complete redemption in glory—the earthly paradise and the heavenly. The two were continually associated in the religious services of the Jews.

When the ancient people were brought out of the house of bondage and a covenant was made with them at Mount Sinai, God ordered a tabernacle or movable tent to be made, where alone the sacrificial services of the Church were to be performed. He gave very explicit directions as to the form of the tent and everything connected with it. It was divided into two apartments, the holy place and the most holy, or holy of holies, or holiest of all. Into the latter only one man, the high priest, was permitted to enter, and he but once a year, on the great day of atonement: "The Holy Ghost this signifying, that the way into the holiest of all was not yet made manifest, while as the first tabernacle was yet standing." Heb. ix. 8. That tabernacle was a symbol of God's perpetual presence with his people. He abode there as their covenant God. There he specially held communion with them. His promise was: "There I will meet with thee, and I will commune with thee from above the mercy-seat." Ex. xxv. 22. The most holy place especially was a type of heaven, and within it were the figures of the cherubim shadowing the mercy-seat, so that the high priest, every time he entered, had his mind pointed back to the paradise which had been lost, and forward to the paradise which was to be entered by redeemed men under the leadership of the great Sacrifice.

After the children of Israel had become fully established in the promised land, a permanent temple was built, and took the place of the movable tabernacle. It was constructed substantially after the same model as that tent. It had the most holy place, under the name of the oracle, the holy place and the outer courts. It was built in Jerusalem, on Mount Moriah, near Mount Zion, on which the royal residence was erected. Jerusalem and Mount Zion then became the centre of the Jewish Church, the peculiar dwelling-place of God. They were a type of heaven because God was there, and the cherubim which pointed forward to heaven as the abode of saved men were there. And so it continued, though the first temple was destroyed and another was built, until Jesus came. He fulfilled in his person and in his work everything that was typified in the temple and its services, and accordingly, some years after his death, God permitted the building to be finally destroyed, the Jews to be scattered and their Church to be broken up, so that never since have their sacrifices been offered.

The Church of God needed no more a local earthly centre, for it was not to be confined to one land, but to cover all the earth. A temple was not needed to be the visible place of God's presence, for Jesus was the true temple in whom the Godhead dwelt; the Son of God became flesh and tabernacled among men. The Church of Christ is now in a peculiar manner the temple of the holy One. No most holy place was any more needed on earth to be entered only once a year; Jesus himself ascended once, for all and for ever, to the heavenly paradise that was shadowed forth by the earthly. He took up with him all that was good about the holy city of the Jews, leaving it only the shadow of a name, and thus the heaven to which he has gone is called the new Jerusalem, the city of our God. That is the capital of our Church, the seat of the divine royalty, the abode of our King-priest. Because the Jerusalem of earth was so long the gracious dwelling-place of God, its associations were so sacred and so delightful that its name came naturally to be applied not merely to the Church, but to its abode in glory—the heavenly paradise—which was expressively symbolized in the most holy place.

With this explanation, let the glory of the heavenly city, as reflected from the enumeration which the inspired apostle gives of its inhabitants, come down upon us.

The paradise which was pointed to even from Eden, and typified in the most holy place of the tabernacle and the temple, we cannot yet see, though it is declared we have come to it. Where, then, is it? A place it is; a particular position it has now. Scarcely anything could teach more strikingly the certainty of that than the apostle's enumeration. But where is it?

There are two ways of answering such a question. In certain circumstances it gives some information of a locality to tell who live in it. Let a father come to this country from the Old World, leaving behind him a babe in its mother's arms. When the child begins to understand what is said to him, he will often hear from his mother about America, where his father is. He will prattle about it whenever a letter reaches his home from his father with some memento for him, and with the means to his mother to bring him hither too. The word "America" will frequently be on his lips. Is he asked what he knows about it and where it is? He cannot tell exactly where, but this he knows: it is the land where his father is, and whither he is soon going to meet him. So it gives us real information about heaven as a place to know what and who are in it.

The other way of answering the question is by giving all the force possible to the expressions of the Bible which seem to indicate the relative locality of paradise in the universe.

The passage that we have quoted from the Epistle to the Hebrews gives an answer in the first of these modes. We proceed to elaborate that in the remainder of this chapter, leaving the second answer, which will endeavor to point to the relative position of the garden-city of glory, to the next chapter.

Paradise, then, is that glorious place in the universe where God has established the throne of his government. "Heaven," says our Lord, "is God's throne." Matt. v. 34. "Thus saith the Lord, The heaven is my throne." Isa. lxvi. 1. Omnipresence is the peculiar attribute of God as the infinite Spirit. There is no place in which it can be declared that he is confined to the exclusion of other places. But the boundless circle of the universe has a centre from which it stretches out in its limitless extent on every side, and there the glory of God is most brilliantly manifested to his creatures.

The vision of this glory bathes the apocalyptic chapters in a peculiar splendor. At the beginning of them, immediately after the reception of the epistles to the seven churches, John declares: "I was in the spirit: and behold a throne was set in heaven, and one sat on the throne. And he that sat was to look upon like a jasper and a sardine stone; and there was a rainbow round about the throne, in sight like unto an emerald." Rev. iv. 2–4. And before that throne "every creature which is in heaven, and on the earth, and such as are in the sea, and all that are in them, heard I saying, Blessing, and honor, and glory, and power be unto him that sitteth upon the throne, and unto the Lamb for ever and ever." Rev. v. 13. Make such descriptions figurative if we will. They represent the peculiar manifestation of the glory, the majesty, the sovereignty, the government, of God. It is not unscriptural to suppose that when God made our world he meant that paradise should be the place of his throne on earth; for when man was banished from the garden, he committed it to cherubim, and the cherubim bear up his throne in its onward progress; but paradise restored, the new Jerusalem, holds that throne still. The throne of God and of the Lamb is in it. It has the glory of God. As it appeared to the inspired seer, it "had no need of the sun, neither of the moon, to shine in it, for the glory of God did lighten it, and the Lamb is the light thereof." Rev. xxi. 22, 23. Ezekiel closed his prophecy by declaring: "The name of the city, from that day, shall be, The Lord is there." And in it alone is literally fulfilled the declaration of the Psalmist: "The Lord hath chosen Zion; he hath desired it for his habitation. This is my rest for ever: here will I dwell; for I have desired it." Ps. cxxxii. 13, 14. The peculiar dwelling-place of God, the seat of his majesty, enlightened by his glory—what a place it is!

"A million torches lighted by thy hand,
Wander unwearied through the blue abyss;
They own thy power, accomplish thy command,
All gay with life, all eloquent with bliss.

What shall we call them? Piles of crystal light,
  A glorious company of golden streams,
Lamps of celestial ether, burning bright,
  Suns lighting systems with their joyous beams:
But thou to these as noon to night." *

How brilliant, then, must be the place of God's immediate presence!

Further, paradise is the place where the glorified Jesus is, with the perfected salvation obtained by the shedding of his infinitely valuable blood. His soul went thither from the cross on the day he died: "*To-day* shalt thou be *with me* in paradise." Paradise is heaven, and before the sun of the crucifixion day went down the soul of Jesus was there. While his body was hanging lifeless on the cross, and while it was lying in Joseph's tomb, the spirit was above with the Father. Just at the moment of death he cried with a loud voice, "Father, into thy hands I commend my spirit: and having said thus, he gave up the ghost."

* Derzhavin, in Book of Poetry (Presbyterian Board of Publication), p. 15.

It is strange that any should suppose that the soul of Jesus between his death and resurrection was anywhere else than with the Father, from whom he had directly come on his mission of salvation.*

* In 1 Peter iii. 18–20 it is declared: "Christ also hath once suffered for sins, the just for the unjust, that he might bring us to God, being put to death in the flesh, but quickened by the spirit: by which also he went and preached unto the spirits in prison, which sometime were disobedient, when once the long-suffering of God waited in the days of Noah, while the ark was a preparing, wherein few, that is, eight souls, were saved by water." To some this seems to teach that the soul of Jesus on his death went to an intermediate place where the spirits of those who died in disobedience in the time of Noah had gone, and that he preached the gospel to them there, and hence that there was a possibility of saving those who had died in their sins. The uniform teaching of the Bible in denial of an intermediate place militates against this interpretation, as does also the declaration that the soul of Jesus was not on his death abandoned to any such place as that to which disobedient spirits go. It is a sound rule of interpretation that an obscure passage of Scripture, which seems to stand alone in teaching a certain dogma, must be explained by the analogy of faith and by other clearer passages.

The explanation usually given of this passage is that Christ, by the Holy Spirit, had preached through Noah to the antediluvians, who, however, persisting in disobedience, were lost, while Noah was saved. The following is suggested in Dr. Fair-

As the soul of Jesus returned from paradise to his body on his resurrection morning, so in the glorified body, on his ascension, he went back to the heavenly place. He is on its throne, and thence he will come at the last day to judgment. His soul went

bairn's chapter on "the Import and Use of Hades in Scripture": As the spirit of Jesus went up from his body, which was left hanging on the cross, its entrance to heaven was perceived not only by the glorified inhabitants of that blessed place, but also by the spirits of the lost who were shut up in their eternal prison, and that was to them not the offer of the gospel salvation—for that is not the meaning of the word translated "preached" in the passage—but a fearful proclamation of their irreparable ruin, since they were out of the blessings of the salvation secured by that death and entrance to glory. If it be asked, Since the world of the lost is so far from heaven as it appears to be represented in the Bible, how could they perceive such an event from such a distance? it may be answered that the perceptive powers of a spirit out of the body cannot be measured by the powers which we now possess. It seems to be the teaching of the Bible that one element of eternal sufferings consists in the sight of the happiness of heaven from which the lost soul is excluded. While there was a great and impassable gulf between the place of the rich man and that of Lazarus, the rich man yet saw Lazarus in Abraham's bosom. And one of the most fearful passages in the book of Revelation declares that the torment of hell is in the presence of the holy angels and of the Lamb. (See pp. 25 and 44, *notes*.)

there from the cross. At the resurrection of the body it came back to earth. For forty days he appeared time and again to his disciples. Then he was received up into heaven and sat on the right hand of God, angels and authorities and powers being made subject unto him. Before his death, to his deeply sorrowing disciples he said: "In my Father's house are many mansions: if it were not so, I would have told you; I go to prepare a place for you." John xiv. 2, 3. There he was seen by the enraptured eye of Stephen, who, while his persecutors were gnashing upon him with their teeth, "being full of the Holy Ghost, looked up steadfastly into heaven, and saw the glory of God, and Jesus standing on the right hand of God, and said, Behold I see the heavens opened, and the Son of man standing on the right hand of God." Acts vii. 55, 56. There he appeared to John, through whom he sends to every soul the message: "To him that overcometh will I grant to sit with me in my throne, even as I also overcame and am set down with my Father in his throne." Rev. iii. 21. And there he is now, in the midst of the throne, a lamb as it had been slain.

> "The head that once was crowned with thorns
> Is crowned with glory now;
> A royal diadem adorns
> The mighty Victor's brow.
>
> "The highest place that heaven affords
> Is his by sovereign right,
> The King of kings and Lord of lords,
> And heaven's eternal light."

It is the presence of Jesus that makes the heaven of the saved soul. Wherever he is is heaven. If we knew nothing more about it, that would be enough. It seems to us that if the place were not indicated in any other mode, or the road not marked to it; if angels were not sent to bear the departing soul aloft, it would yet quickly, by the force of a celestial gravitation, urge its way through the mazes of infinite space at once to the foot of the Redeemer's throne. The enrapturing brilliancy of his glorified form would draw it on. When the Spirit of Jesus comes to the soul, the heaven of grace comes to it; when the soul goes to the glorified Jesus, it enters the heaven of glory.

Again, paradise is the place where the angels of God are. It is their home. "The angels do there," said Christ, "always behold the face of my Father." Matt. xviii. 10. Thence Gabriel came forth to make Daniel understand the vision which he had seen. Thence he came again to announce to Zacharias the birth of John, and to Mary the birth of Jesus. Thence the angel of the Lord came upon the shepherds, while the glory of the Lord shone round about them, and announced the advent of the Saviour, Christ the Lord. Sent forth as ministering spirits to minister to the heirs of salvation, continually passing between heaven and earth on their errands of mercy, bending with interest over every church where the gospel is preached, and every place where the word of God is read or a word spoken for Jesus, and waiting for occasions of renewed joy in the repentance of sinners, paradise is the place to which the angels ever return. They are the elder brothers of that blissful home. Together with the redeemed they bend before the same throne, and with them adore the same crucified yet triumphant Lamb, and unite with them in some of their songs; for the beloved disciple declares: "I beheld, and I heard the voice of many angels round about the throne, and the living creatures, and the elders, and the number of them was ten thousand times ten thousand, and thousands of thousands; saying with a loud voice, Worthy is the Lamb that was slain to receive power, and riches, and wisdom, and strength, and honor, and glory, and blessing." Rev. v. 11, 12. What a city must that be where angels minister to saved souls—where those who have never fallen are companions of redeemed sinners!

Paradise is also the place where the Church of the first-born and the spirits of the just made perfect are. By the first class is probably meant Old Testament believers, those who died before the coming of Christ; by the second, those who had died between that and the writing of the epistle, to whom we may now add all the redeemed that have died since and at their death were made perfect in holiness.

On the day of his death Jesus entered paradise, and it is the great happiness of all his people to go at the instant of their death to the very place where he is. "If I go and prepare a place for you, I will come again and receive you unto myself; that where I am there ye may be also." John xiv. 3. None of them are long absent from his glorious abode after they have believed in him, for he comes to them at death; and the longest life that is spent in his service on earth is less than an instant compared with eternity. "If any man serve me let him follow me; and where I am there shall also my servant be." John xii. 26. "Now, Father, come I to thee." And "I will that they also whom thou hast given me be with me where I am; that they may behold my glory which thou hast given me." John xvii. 13, 24. The glory of heaven comes down to the death-bed of the believer. The Holy Spirit is there; ministering angels are there; and ere the body has ceased to quiver in the throes of death the soul is borne aloft to the glory of the golden city, where are living all the glorified redeemed from Abel down to the unknown saint that may just this hour have breathed his last on earth.

What a soul-thrilling place, then, that city is! The capital of the universe, the centre of creation, elevated above the shifting scenes of time, far removed from the sinful imperfections of earth, it is the region to which, through the films of sin and of sorrow, the purged eye of the believer ever looks. The home of earth's redeemed sinners; the Mount Zion of the skies; the new Jerusalem of our God to which the tribes go up; the seat of royalty from which God gives his laws and to which he draws his chosen,—glorious things are spoken of the city of our God. No mean city is it; no small spot in the universe; no obscure region; no out-of-the-way place. It must be the most prominent and the most favored part of creation. It is large, and already it is immensely populous. Its inhabitants are literally innumerable. It received some of them before this world was made. From the death of Abel down to this hour its pearly gates have never been shut. Through them the redeemed pilgrims of earth have ever been pressing. "And the nations of them which are saved walk in the light of it; and the kings of the earth do bring their glory and honor into it." Rev. xxi. 24. Nothing that defileth or worketh abomination or maketh a lie has ever entered there; but those who are written in the Lamb's book of life, embracing all the really good and honorable in the nations, are received into it. "Are there few that be saved?" (Luke xiii. 23) a speculative curiosity once asked of Jesus. His practical answer was, "Strive to enter in at the strait gate." But elsewhere we have the assurance that the redeemed are "a great multitude which no man can number of all nations, and kindreds, and peoples, and tongues." Rev. vii. 9. Our whole world—its present population of more than a thousand million souls—is but a little hamlet compared with the mighty population that is already in the city of our God; and yet there is room for more.*

* There are some perversions and misrepresentations of our old orthodox system of doctrine which are perpetually circulated and repeated against all denials. One of the most threadbare and yet persistently rewoven of these theological slanders is the charge that our "Confession" teaches the eternal condemnation of those who die in infancy and the salvation of a very small proportion of the human race. But on this point Dr. Charles

The evangelical prophet Isaiah saw the glory of the redeeming Son of God in the heavenly place before his incarnation, and thus he described it: "I saw the Lord sitting upon a throne high and lifted up, and his train filled the temple. Above it stood the seraphims: each one had six wings: with twain he covered his face, and with twain he covered his feet, and with twain he did fly. And one cried unto another, and said, Holy, holy, holy is the Lord of hosts; the whole earth is full of his glory." But the effect upon the prophet was that he

Hodge has unequivocally (in his "Systematic Theology," i. 26) expressed our belief: "The Scriptures nowhere exclude any class of infants, baptized or unbaptized, born in Christian or heathen lands, of believing or unbelieving parents, from the benefits of the redemption of Christ. All the descendants of Adam except Christ are under condemnation; all the descendants of Adam, except those of whom it is expressly revealed that they cannot inherit the kingdom of God, are saved. This appears to be the clear meaning of the apostle in Rom. v. 18, 19, and therefore he does not hesitate to say that where sin abounded grace has much more abounded, that the benefits of redemption far exceed the evils of the fall, that *the number of the saved far exceeds the number of the lost.*"

cried out: "Woe is me! for I am undone: because I am a man of unclean lips, and I dwell in the midst of a people of unclean lips: for mine eyes have seen the King, the Lord of hosts." Isa. vi. 1–6.

Peter, James and John also saw that glory in the mount of transfiguration, when the face of Jesus did shine as the sun, and his raiment was white as the light, and the Shekinah came down from heaven, and a voice was heard saying, This is my beloved Son; but they fell on their faces and were sore afraid, and wist not what to say.

On the road to Damascus, Paul was bathed in the glory of the ascended Lord, which, pouring down from the great white throne with its rainbow halo, outshone the burning splendor of the noonday sun; but it blinded the persecutor. When, in the apocalyptic vision, John saw it, it made him fall at the feet of Jesus as dead. Not until made perfectly holy can any man look for an instant upon the direct glory of the place. But through the revealed word we see it dimly, and that view should be enough to make us yearn after a full preparation for the enjoyment of it.

What heart is so cold, so unmoved by the brightness of the original inhabitants of our paradise and of the long procession of saints who for six thousand years have been marching over the highway of our God from earth to heaven, and entering the charmed circle of the great white throne, and who are now beckoning to us that are still behind to follow,—what heart is so unruffled as not to cry out?—

> "For thee, O dear, dear country,
> Mine eyes their vigils keep;
> For very love beholding
> Thy happy name they weep.
> The mention of thy glory
> Is unction to the breast,
> And medicine in sickness,
> And love and life and rest."

Who is there that, while deriving comfort from the scene and looking forward with eager hope to a final entrance to it through grace, will not under its influence seek after a holier conformity to its life?

The children of Israel, after their deliverance from the house of bondage, came to Mount Sinai, which burned and sparkled and flashed with the terrors of the Lord. The mountain might be touched, but they dare not come near to it. We have come to Mount Zion, and unto the city of the living God, the new Jerusalem. We cannot see it. In space it seems to be far away. Yet it is so near to the saved that the liberated soul in an instant reaches it from the body, and its inhabitants and believers on earth form one family, one Church, one kingdom. We have come to it. But no terrors surround it—no gloom or blackness, no darkness or tempest. All about it is gentle, attractive, winning. Its foundations of precious stones; its gates of pearls; its street of pure gold, as transparent glass; its river of life as clear as crystal; the light of the whole like unto a jasper stone; the everlasting prevalence of day through its pure and healthy atmosphere; the absence of pain and sorrow and crying from its borders,—these descriptions excel all human imagination and stir our hearts to their depths.

But more than all, God our Father, and Christ our Redeemer, and the unfallen angels, and the whole army of the redeemed who have already been arrayed in robes made perfectly white in the blood of the Lamb, are in the glorious place, and we, humble believers in the Lord, hope ere long to mingle in their society. They belong to us and we belong to them, and the new Jerusalem is their and our home.

What happiness is in store for us! What a high calling we have! Let us seek to walk worthy of it; and remembering that they who are above and we who are still on the earth are closely joined together, let us strive to live the life of heaven while we are here. Let us feel the throbbings of its great heart. Let its life pulsate through our lives. Let the atmosphere of the blessed city settle down upon our daily walk, and pervade our homes, and inspire our souls. Let us, through a lively faith in the crucified One, seek to die daily unto sin, and to live unto righteousness, so that we may the more and more anticipate the perfect holiness and the exalted communion and the ineffable happiness of the glorious city.

CHAPTER IV.

THE LOCALITY OF PARADISE.

PARADISE is heaven. Heaven is the place where the throne of God, the glorified Jesus, the angels and the spirits of the just made perfect are. It is a particular place now existing in the universe; Enoch and Elijah long ago took their bodies thither. But what has been revealed to us as to its precise locality?

1. The Bible uniformly represents it as being *away from the earth*. "Elijah went up by a whirlwind into heaven." 2 Kings ii. 11. It would scarcely be necessary to make this remark but for the purpose of adding to it another. Paradise is so far and so completely separated from us, that

the glorified spirits of the redeemed have no communication with the earth in its present form and dispensation. We have no reason to think that the human inhabitants of heaven are now in any way within the range of this world, or hover about it at any time or in any form.

A considerable amount of Christian sentimentality exists on this point. Apart from the destructive error which represents departed spirits as holding communications, in a material manner, with persons who are still on the earth, there is, perhaps, in many Christian minds, an undefined idea that the spirits of their friends may at times be near them, though they can make no revelations to them. But there is one fact which bears with great force against this notion.

To say nothing of the communications made to man before the time of Moses, many of which are preserved in the inspired book of Genesis, the period which extended from the writing of that book down to the composition of the Apocalypse, which wound up the circle of miraculous communications, embraced nearly sixteen hundred years. That was the age of revelations from heaven to earth. Communications were frequent and many. But through all those years human spirits were not sent by God from heaven to make known his will, to tell about heaven, to foretell the future, to hold converse of any kind with men. Angels very often came down with communications from the Lord. Supernatural visions were granted to holy men, who were inspired by God to write the sacred books. Jesus Christ appeared on earth and instructed men, and after his ascension from the earth made further disclosures through the inspired writers. But human spirits were not in the habit of coming back from their happy abode to communicate with the men they had left behind.

There are only two apparent exceptions to this statement. At the transfiguration of Christ, Moses and Elijah appeared with him in glory, and spake of the decease which he should accomplish at Jerusalem; but if the three disciples understood, they did not record, what was said; and even that appearance had a design that permits no repetition. In his judicial blindness, Saul the king demanded of the woman of Endor that she should bring up Samuel to him, and the account is given of what purported to be an apparition from the spirit-world to the wretched man. But it is the opinion of many of the thoughtful, from a careful examination of the narrative, that the whole transaction was a delusion. It is not evident that the king saw Samuel. It is nowhere said that he did see the prophet, though the woman described what she pretended she saw in such a way as to make Saul recognize the description, and he "perceived that it was Samuel." As in many other cases in the Bible, the interview, with the pretence on the woman's part, is reported without comment, leaving that to be drawn from the result. But if that were a real appearance and communication, it is not one that would commend the matter to us, for it was permitted as a punishment and it foretold only evil.*

* The Scripture narrative, as is well said in Dr. Wm. Smith's *Old Testament History*, p. 350, "certainly conveys the impression that there was a real apparition in the form of Samuel, and that the words heard by Saul were uttered by the spectre. But when we remember that the Scripture relates things as they appear to the witnesses, without necessarily implying their reality, the question still remains whether the apparition was real or an imposture. On this point opinions have been divided in every age." (The most of the Fathers considered it an imposture.) "All the analogy of experience, all the deductions of reasoning and all the general lessons of Scripture unite in branding every form of magic and necromancy as an imposture; and the safest conclusion is to reject every claim to supernatural power or knowledge in any other form than as a revelation from God himself, from the arts of the Egyptian priests and the oracles of the Greeks down to the pitiful absurdities which find credence in our own day." In reference to the conversation that appeared to take place

The heathen thought that in dreams spirits came back to them from their abode in the other world. "Thus Homer represents that Achilles first became convinced that

between Samuel and Saul while the latter stooped with his face to the ground, it is worthy of notice that the expression in 1 Sam. xxviii. 7, "a woman that hath a familiar spirit," is literally "a woman mistress of Ob," which the Septuagint explains as a ventriloquist. On the other hand, *The Annotated Paragraph Bible* of the London Religious Tract Society (we believe by Dr. Angus) contains the following suggestive note *in loc.*: "The clear and decided language of the passage forbids us to suppose that all this was a mere imposture practiced by the woman, with or without demoniacal aid, and the teachings of Scripture respecting the limited power of Satan do not agree with the notion that Samuel was actually called up by such agency. We must, therefore, regard this as a divine interposition, unexpected by both parties, either producing miraculously an impression upon the senses of Saul and the woman, which is not impossible, or causing the real presence of Samuel, which, when a miracle is admitted, presents no greater difficulties, agrees more naturally with the language (for there is no intimation that the whole was a vision), and is analogous to the resuscitation of which we read elsewhere. (See Matt. xxvii. 52, 53.) Thus Saul was rebuked for his new crime, whilst, like Pharaoh, he received a last solemn warning on the eve of his destruction. It should be observed that the answer of Samuel was fulfilled to the letter, and was anything but such as the woman would have been likely to give."

souls and shadowy forms have a real existence in the kingdom of the shades by the appearance to him of the departed Patroclus in a dream." An apostate Church has worked upon the fears and the excited imaginations of its deluded votaries by the pretended reappearance of saints clothed even in bodily forms before their resurrection. But the Bible not merely places the glorified souls far away from the earth, with its sins and sorrows, but gives no countenance to the idea that they ever come across the deep profound that separates their present abode from their late dwelling-place. In heaven they remain, and shall remain until they come again with Christ at the last day to receive their bodies redeemed and glorified.

2. Paradise is, in the language of the Bible, *above* the earth: "John bare record, saying, I saw the Spirit *descending* from heaven like a dove." John i. 32. "No man hath *ascended up* to heaven, but he that *came*

down from heaven." John iii. 13. "After this I looked, and behold a door was opened in heaven: and the first voice which I heard was as it were of a trumpet talking with me, which said, *Come up hither.*" Rev. iv. 1. "And they heard a great voice from heaven, saying unto them, *Come up hither.* And they *ascended up* to heaven in a cloud." Rev. xi. 12.

The earth is a sphere or globe. When we speak of heaven and point upward, and when an inhabitant directly opposite to us on the earth speaks of it and points upward, we point in diametrically opposite directions. We seem to look to heaven as one place, and yet as situated in different quarters of the universe. This is adduced by some as an exhibition of a want of scientific accuracy in the Bible, while others say that the expression simply indicates that heaven is a most exalted place. The latter explanation is a true one. We speak of *looking up* to a man who occupies a higher position in the world than we do. He is said to be above us. In this way also the abode of the glorified redeemed is a far more exalted place than this earth.

But, after all, this scriptural expression is, in a physical point of view, more accurate than some of its impugners would imagine. We have never met, outside of the holy book, with a passage which gives a more striking view of the immensity of the universe, and of course of the infinity and power of God who made it, while it also brings out the idea that we intend to convey on this point, than an extract from a German writer. He embodies his instructions in the form of a dream, which of course is imaginary, but the truth remains grand and sublime:

"God called up from dreams a man into the vestibule of heaven, saying, Come thou hither and see the glory of my house. And to the servants that stood around his throne he said, Take him and undress him from his robes of flesh; cleanse his vision and put new breath into his nostrils; only touch not with any change his human heart, the heart that weeps and trembles. It was done; and with a mighty angel for his guide, the man stood ready for his infinite voyage; and from the terrace of heaven, without sound or farewell, at once they wheeled away into endless space. Sometimes with the solemn flight of angel wing they fled through Saharas of darkness, through wildernesses of death that divided the worlds of life; sometimes they swept over frontiers that were quickening under prophetic motions from God. Then, from a distance that is counted only in heaven, light dawned for a time through a sleepy film; by unutterable pace the light swept to them, they by unutterable pace to the light. In a moment the rushing of planets was upon them; in a moment the blazing of suns was around them. Then came eternities of twilight that revealed, but were not revealed. On the right hand and on the left towered mighty constellations that by self-repetitions and answers from afar, that by counter-positions built up by triumphal gates whose architraves, whose archways, horizontal, upright, rested, rose, at altitude by spans that seemed ghostly from infinitude. Without measure were the architraves, past number were the archways, beyond memory the gates. Within were stairs that scaled eternities below; *above was below, below was above, to the man stripped of gravitating body;* depth was swallowed up in height insurmountable; height was swallowed up in depth unfathomable. Suddenly, as thus they rode from infinite to infinite, as thus they tilted over abysmal worlds, a mighty cry arose that systems more mysterious, that worlds more billowy, other heights and other depths, were coming, were near, were at hand." *

* Richter; quoted by O. M. Mitchell in his "Planetary and Stellar Worlds," p. 287.

In the immense circle of the universe, which is ever returning on itself, below is above and above is below to the man stripped of a gravitating body. So small is this world and such its position in the infinite that souls in bounding from its surface, no matter from what side, as they quickly pass from its immediate region, go up the one line to reach the heaven they are bound for.

3. The apostle Paul calls paradise the "*third heaven.*" 2 Cor. xii. 2. That means the highest heaven. The first heaven, according to the Jewish idea, was the aërial heaven, the region of the atmosphere where the birds fly, the winds blow and the clouds are formed. The second was the firmament, or starry heavens, wherein the heavenly bodies are disposed. The third was the highest heaven, the place of God's residence, and the dwelling of the angels and the blessed saints. Thus paradise is declared to be *above the clouds and beyond the*

visible expanse or the firmament of stars. At his ascension a cloud received Jesus out of the sight of his disciples. Acts i. 9. "Thou hast said in thine heart, I will ascend into heaven; I will exalt my throne above the stars of God; I will sit upon the mount of the congregation, in the sides of the north; I will ascend above the clouds; I will be like the Most High." Isa. xiv. 13. The clouds are declared to be the dust of God's feet.* Nah. i. 3. When Jesus was baptized, the heavens were opened unto him, and he saw the Spirit of God descending like a dove and lighting upon him, and, lo! a voice from heaven saying, This is my beloved Son, in whom I am well pleased. In the presence of the Jewish Sanhedrim Stephen declared, Behold I see the heav-

* We think we never fully realized the force and beauty of this expression until a recent ascent of the White Mountains. As we slowly wound our way up to the summit we passed through the clouds, and then, when we reached the top, we beheld them floating below us, in many places looking really like a fine dust filling the air

ens opened and the Son of man standing on the right hand of God.

In these cases there was "an apparent separation or division of the visible expanse of heaven," * as if in the one to afford a passage to the form and voice which are mentioned as coming down from heaven, and in the other to enable the first martyr to see the place where our Redeemer was and whither he was himself going.

The prophets make use of the expression "the opening of the heavens" to signalize special revelations coming from God who dwells above. Thus Ezekiel opens his book with the declaration that the heavens were opened and he saw visions of God. And Isaiah cries out: "Oh that thou wouldst rend the heavens, that thou wouldst come down, that the mountains might flow down at thy presence as when the melting fire burneth, the fire causeth the waters to boil, to make thy name

* Dr. J. Addison Alexander on Mark i. 10.

known to thine adversaries, that the nations may tremble at thy presence." Isa. lxiv. 1.

Certainly, then, above all that the naked eye of the writers of the Bible could discover, is the paradise to which saved souls go at death.

4. Moreover, it is *far above* all these things. The apostle Paul declares that when Jesus went up "he ascended far above all heavens that he might fill all things." Eph. iv. 10. Away beyond the limits of the visible creation, as the naked eye of man can take it in, God seems to have established the paradise where our glorified Jesus now is with the departed souls of the saved.

More definitely than this the Scriptures do not reveal the locality. Therefore we must be reverent and humble in our thoughts about it. What we think or what we say must not be advanced as a dogmatic utterance. To muse upon it is natural. If it were God's will, we would all doubtless like to know exactly where the place is. But he has not made it known, and anything that may be advanced about it must be received as a surmise until death come and take us to the place. In ancient times it was conceived of as the whole expanse of heaven, high above the atmosphere or starry region. Some modern writers think of it as a particular planet or world. It is safe to assume that it must be a place of peculiar brightness. In the account which Paul gave to King Agrippa of his conversion he declared: "At midday, O king! I saw in the way a light from heaven, above the brightness of the sun, shining round about me and them which journeyed with me." Acts xxvi. 13. Did not the heavens, then, open, and did not the light of paradise shine down upon the traveler? True, it was the Shekinah, the glory of God, that surrounded him, but that is the light of heaven.

As we muse upon this most interesting subject our minds go up and our thoughts expand until we are lost in admiration at the immensity of heaven and the greatness of our God and Redeemer, who has peopled it with its world inhabitants. If we fail in exactly localizing paradise, we are yet sure that it is the most beautiful, the most delightful, the most alluring place in all the universe.

But in our musings the question addressed by God to Job arrests us: "Canst thou bind the sweet influences of Pleiades?" This is the name of a constellation in the northern part of the heavens. The Hebrew word thus rendered means literally a *hinge, pivot, axle*, which turns around and moves other bodies along with it. As we ponder the question we are reminded that astronomy has discovered that Alcyone, the brightest star of the Pleiades, is the centre of gravitation of our vast solar system, the luminous hinge in the heavens around which our sun and his attendant planets are moving through space.

That sun of ours is not stationary. Our world, revolving daily on its own axis, revolves also yearly round him; and he and all the system of worlds dependent upon him move slowly round that constellation Pleiades; and to that revolution "is due indirectly and in a higher sense than that of the old astrological belief the beautiful and grateful vicissitudes of the seasons on our earth. . . .

In the vast and complex arrangements by which worlds on worlds thus revolve round and through each other, "not one wheel jars or creaks, not a single discordant sound disturbs the deep, solemn quietude of the midnight sky. Smoothly and silently each star performs its sublime revolutions. . . . Moons revolve round planets, comets and planets round the sun, the sun around Alcyone, and Alcyone round some other unknown sun hidden far away in some unexplored depths of our galaxy; and, grand beyond conception, this cluster of systems round the great centre of ten thousand centres, the white throne of the Eternal and the Infinite, and all with rhythm so perfect that we might almost believe in the old poetic fable of 'the music of the spheres.'"

The heavenly movements are majestic; but we look for Him who presides over them. And "in this vision of orbs and revolutions, more awful and stupendous than Ezekiel's vision of wheels within wheels, we see on the throne above the firmament, not a blind chance or a passionless fate, but one like unto the Son of man, he whom John saw in Patmos, holding the mystery of the seven stars in his right hand, possessed of infinite love as well as infinite power, binding and loosing the sweet influences of Pleiades solely for the good of his creation." *

In a particular place, on the throne of the universe, at present hidden away in the

* *Sunday Magazine*, vol. i., pp. 442, 443.

depths of the infinite and among those mighty constellations, is our Redeemer, ruling over all worlds, but bending upon our earth a peculiarly sympathetic eye. That place is the paradise where all the departed spirits of the saved now are; and thither, if we may be permitted through a penitent faith in Jesus to indulge the hope, we shall go at the moment of death.

At the very moment of death all souls pass immediately from earth either to heaven or hell, between which places there is no communication. The redeemed go at once from the body to Jesus in heaven without delaying in any intermediate spot. What could be more direct on this than the assertion of Christ to the dying penitent? On the day of his death he was with the Redeemer in paradise. As soon as Lazarus died his soul was carried by angels to Abraham in heaven. Paul declares, "We know that if our earthly house of this tabernacle were dissolved we have" (not we shall have, but at the moment of dissolution we have) "a house not made with hands, eternal in the heavens." "Therefore," he adds, "we are always confident, knowing that whilst we are at home in the body, we are absent from the Lord," and we are "willing rather to be absent from the body and present with the Lord." 2 Cor. v. 1, 6–8. The soul out of the body is in heaven with its Lord. Therefore the great working apostle could say again, "To me to live is Christ and to die is gain;" and "I am in a strait betwixt two, having a desire to depart and be with Christ, which is far better." Phil. i. 21, 23.

As we stand at the bedside of a dying Christian and see in the tremor of the body its sense of the soul fluttering away from it, we love to think that even before the corpse has become entirely cold, while it is still quivering under the forcible departure of the spirit from it, the soul itself is already with the glorified Jesus. It ascends to its abode of holiness and happiness more quickly than the body goes to its bed of earth.

Does this startle any when they think of the immense distance at which paradise seems to be placed from the earth? Let us cease to judge of the power of the disembodied spirit by its motions whilst it is clogged in the natural body of earth. God himself, the great Spirit, is everywhere at all times. With him distance is not. The angels are continually passing from heaven to earth and back again on God's work; and their speed may be so great in their transitions from one to the other that "far as the regions may be asunder they may make the passage quick as a gleam of lightning and rapid as the twinkling of an eye." Liberated souls may be borne aloft as quickly. And once in heaven they remain there, far away from this earth until it shall be regenerated and purified by the great conflagration of the last day. Then they will return; "for if we believe that Jesus died and rose again, even so them also which sleep in Jesus will God bring with him." 1 Thess. iv. 14. They will come to reclaim their bodies from the grave and to reassume them in a glorified form like the glorified body of Christ; and after that the seat of their kingdom may be changed.

We are strenuous in guarding against the idea of any intermediate place between heaven and earth where the righteous do not enjoy perfect bliss. "The souls of believers are at their death made perfect in holiness and do immediately pass into glory eternal and a high degree of happiness." As to a change of locality at the judgment day, "whether the righteous and wicked after the judgment go literally to the same place in which they were before situated, it is not material to inquire; but both before and after the judgment the righteous will be in the same place with their glorified Saviour and his holy angels, and this will be heaven; and before and after the judgment the wicked will be in the same place with the devil and his angels, and this will be hell."

But if we read the Bible aright on this point, after the purification of our globe by fire and after the judgment day, the heaven of Christ's redeemed people will be transferred to this earth in its renovated and glorified form. This seems to be the truth which John teaches in the twenty-first chapter of his Revelation. He saw a new heaven and a new earth, for the first heaven and the first earth were passed away, and there was no more sea. That new heaven and new earth the apostle Peter declares will be the result of the great conflagration. 2 Pet. iii. And then John adds: "I saw the holy city, new Jerusalem, coming down from God out of heaven prepared as a bride adorned for her husband;" and again: "And he carried me away in the spirit to a great and high mountain, and showed me that great city, the holy Jerusalem, descending out of heaven from God, having the glory of God."

The view which has been exhibited of the paradise of the redeemed brings it very near to us. It is just on the other side of death. And death is not far off; it is passing by us every day; it is seizing one soul after another; and it will lay its hand upon us very soon, very suddenly, perhaps ere we are aware. But let heaven be brought nearer still to us. It is not merely a future place, but a present state. "The kingdom of heaven is within you." Luke xvii. 21. It consists "in righteousness, peace, and joy in the Holy Ghost." Rom. xiv. 17. The heaven of grace must enter our souls here, or we cannot enter the heaven of glory hereafter. Paradise is a place of exceeding beauty, but its highest beauty is its holiness. That is the atmosphere of the place; and holy we must become through the sanctifying influence of the Spirit of God, or we can never enjoy it. While, then, the imagination is captivated by the beautiful descriptions of the Bible, let us seek to be brought under the influence of the holy One. As we gaze upon the glory of heaven, as we peer away through the distance that stretches between us and the place, let us ponder the Saviour's declaration that except we be born again we cannot see it. Let us not forget that we must be justified by Christ and sanctified by the Spirit in order to enter there; and let us remember that the hour is at hand when from the throne will sound in the dying ear the sentence: "He that is unjust, let him be unjust still: and he which is filthy, let him be filthy still: and he that is righteous, let him be righteous still: and he that is holy, let him be holy still." Rev. xxii. 11.

Those whom death finds unholy cannot enter heaven. Therefore, bow before the Redeemer with the petition of a penitent faith: "Renew a right spirit within me." Ps. li. 10. Seek daily to grow in grace. Then, let death come when and how it will, life may be closed with the quiet, confident, triumphant prayer, "Lord Jesus, receive my spirit" (Acts vii. 59); and immediately the soul shall bound aloft quicker than the sunbeam, to the great white throne and to the personal and bodily presence of Him who gives fullness of joy, and to his right hand, where pleasures throb and surge and enrapture for evermore.

CHAPTER V.

THE STATE OF SOULS IN PARADISE.

THE Sadducees, who denied the doctrine of the resurrection, once undertook to puzzle our Lord and to insinuate a "grave scoff" at the truth which they rejected. Luke xx. 27–38. They quoted a regulation of the Mosaic law which is recorded in Deut. xxv. 5–10, and which was of a temporary character for the purpose of preserving the tribes of Israel in their distinct existence. The quibblers started a fictitious and, we may say, an improbable case under that law. It is not likely that it ever had been a fact; and they asked in a sneering tone, If this woman and her seven husbands rise again in the body of which of the seven shall she be the wife? In reply the divine Teacher corrected the low and carnal construction which the question put on the resurrection by declaring that after that event, as the inhabitants of the sinless land cannot possibly die, so there will be no such thing as marriage and propagation to make up for death. This is one respect in which the spiritual body, while the same as the natural body, will differ from it. Then the blessed Master, speaking with the authority which belonged to him, asserted that the bodily resurrection is really involved in true views of the existence of the soul; and because of the union between the spiritual and the physical in man, as the one lives on for ever, the other must rise from the grave to make the person complete. The proof of it is this: Moses wrote that, hundreds of years after the death of Abraham, Isaac and Jacob, God declared: "*I am* their God," showing that they were still living after their physical death. "To you," inti mates the Saviour—"to you, skeptical Sad-ducees, that may seem to be a mere reminiscence of the past; but I can tell you that the patriarchs are there referred to not as persons who exist no longer, nor even as disembodied spirits, but as living men possessed of souls and bodies, whose God Jehovah is to be for ever—a relation partially suspended for the present by the separation of those parts, but hereafter to be fully reinstated by the resurrection and redemption of the body." * And this, which was true of the patriarchs, is true of all, "for all live unto God." They are all immortal. They do not, like brutes, die when their bodies are decomposed in the grave. They are not annihilated. They continue to live under the control of God.

This grand declaration of the infallible One introduces us to the life of saved

* Dr. J A. Alexander *in loco.*

souls, while out of their bodies, in the paradise whither they are translated immediately from their earthly abode.

1. That life continues to be a distinct individual life. The souls of the saved, as they go from their bodies to heaven, retain their separate existence, their personality. Here their residence in visible bodies marks off the distinction of souls from each other, and it might, therefore, occur to some that when they pass from their earthly tenements into the widely-peopled spirit-world they may in some way lose that distinction and be confused with others. But "when the dust returns to the earth as it was, the spirit returns to God who gave it—not, as some have dreamed, to be reabsorbed by the divine essence from which it originally emanated, but, continuing to preserve its separate being, to enter on a new form of existence." Its individuality does not disappear in the divine essence, nor is it lost in the maze of universal existence.

In the account of the restoration to life of the son of the widow of Zarephath it is said that Elijah the prophet "stretched himself upon the child three times, and cried unto the Lord and said, O Lord my God, I pray thee let this child's soul come into him again," or, as it is in the margin of the Bible, "into his inward parts." "And the Lord heard the voice of Elijah; and the soul of the child came into him again, and he revived." 1 Kings xvii. 21, 22. When Jesus took the dead daughter of Jairus by the hand and said, "Maid, arise," "her spirit came again, and she arose straightway." Luke viii. 55. Akin to this is the declaration of Paul: "For we know that if our earthly house of this tabernacle were dissolved, we have a building of God, a house not made with hands, eternal in the heavens." 2 Cor. v. 1.

There is a philosophic heresy which teaches that the soul is not a being entirely distinct in substance from matter, but only the result of our peculiar bodily organization, and that when the body decays and is disorganized what is called the soul ceases to exist, until the body is reorganized again in a similar way to result in thinking.

This low materialistic notion floats about a good deal in the current and popular literature of the day. The passages just quoted from the Bible show that it recognizes no such dogma. They draw a sharp distinction between the human spirit and the body, intimately united though they are, for the spirit is spoken of under the figure of an inmate inhabiting the body as a temporary earthly tenement. They also point to the continued separate existence of the soul in a personal condition after death; for if the spirit goes away from the body and can come back to it as it did in those cases, the inference is unquestionable that in the mean time it continues to exist somewhere else in as perfectly distinct and individual a mode as it did while in the body—an inference which is placed beyond all doubt by the parable of Dives and Lazarus and by the temporary reappearance in glory of Moses and Elijah at the transfiguration of Christ.

In the present stage of our existence the clearly-defined bodily form marks off each individual from all others. In the heavenly world each soul, while out of the body, is to other spiritual intelligences as distinctly divided from its fellows. Immediately at death it leaves the earth and takes its station near the throne in the glorious light of God's countenance, and amid the spiritual blaze of heaven. In the highest sense it then becomes perfectly a partaker of the divine nature. But "as the air when thoroughly illumined by sunshine still keeps its aërial nature and does not become sunshine, or as iron all red in the flame still keeps its metallic substance and does not turn to fire itself, so a soul fully possessed and moved by God does not in consequence lose its own sentient and intelligent being." It is still a being of distinct existence, with its own thoughts and feelings and volitions separate from all others. Thus disembodied spirits can recognize each other. A living English poet has most beautifully sung this Christian truth:

"That each who seems a separate whole
Should move his rounds, and fusing all
The skirts of self again should fall
Remerging in the general soul,

"Is faith as vague as all unsweet:
Eternal form shall still divide
The eternal soul from all beside,
And I shall know him when we meet."

How exceedingly splendid must the appearance of the soul be! If the glory of heaven transfigured the body of our Lord even while he was on the earth, so that the fashion of his countenance was altered and his raiment was white and glistering,—if after he ascended to the brilliant land his countenance was as the sun shineth in his strength,—

and if his people after the resurrection day shall wear bodies like unto his glorious body, —may we not rest assured that as the soul, which is to have such a resplendent eternal abode, passes from the earthly tabernacle in which it is now confined, it appears a shining and brilliant being? We know not now what a human spirit is like, for it is "cabined, cribbed, confined" in an imperfect sinful body; nor can we imagine, and perhaps just as little could any of us yet gaze upon, the glorious appearance which the translated souls wear in the better land.

2. The life of the blessed souls in paradise is an unceasingly active life. As they pass into their intermediate state they not only retain their separate personality, but they continue unceasingly active in it. We look upon a body just after it has died, and we behold it entirely motionless. It can be moved, but it cannot move itself. Naturally the question arises, Is the soul which

has passed out of this tenement also in a passive condition? Wherever it may be, is it as quiet and motionless as the physical frame is? And perhaps the first prompting is to think, as even some Christian writers do think, that the rest into which the immortal spirit has entered may be somewhat similar to the passive rest of its earthly tabernacle.

Such an idea, however, should not be entertained. The human spirit not only continues to exist after the death of the body, but the consciousness of its life is unbroken and unsuspended for a single instant. The soul never becomes insensible. It never sleeps. It never ceases to be active. Neither at death nor at any subsequent period is there a suspension of rational life, or a weakening of its powers, or a failure to connect the past with the present existence. The spirit continues to think and feel and act without intermission. Above all, the new and higher life which is communicated in regeneration exists on through death without any break; and this carries along with it the continued exercise and enjoyment of that life. The spiritual part of the believer neither dies, sleeps, nor becomes inactive for one instant.

This is involved in what Paul declares: "If Christ be in you, the body is dead because of sin; but the spirit"—that is, in this passage, the human spirit—"is life because of righteousness." Rom. viii. 10. The body shall die, but the soul shall continue to live; it is itself life. Life in such a manner belongs to it that unless we think of it as entirely blotted out of being into nothingness, which is impossible, we must conceive of it as retaining all its energies without any cessation. Bodily death is a part of the world's curse from which not even the justified believer is freed, though at the resurrection it shall be overcome: from the spiritual and eternal death of the soul he is delivered when the Holy Spirit takes up his abode in him; and then on, on, for ever and ever, through this life, through physical death and through eternity, his life glows and burns, never going out, never growing dim.

This truth is also asserted in the declaration of the Redeemer: "Verily, verily, I say unto you, He that heareth my word and believeth on him that sent me, hath everlasting life, and shall not come into condemnation, but is passed from death unto life." John v. 24. And how cheeringly does it ring through what is perhaps the most heart-stirring of all Christ's declarations! "I am the resurrection and the life: he that believeth in me, though he were dead, yet shall he live: and whosoever liveth and believeth in me shall never die." John xi. 25, 26. Not only shall the dead body live again when the archangel's trump shall be heard sounding through the graves of earth, but the soul which is born anew in this life, and lives and believes, shall never die; and as the essential idea of life is activity, there shall be no suspension in its powers of action.

Here also comes in Paul's strong expression of his faith: "For God hath not appointed us to wrath, but to obtain salvation by our Lord Jesus Christ, who died for us, that whether we wake or sleep," whether in the body we live or die, "we should live together with him." 1 Thess. v. 9, 10.

Take away this truth from the fifth chapter of Second Corinthians, and the peculiar force of that comforting chapter is destroyed.

Without this what would become of Paul's declaration to the Philippians: "To me to live is Christ, and to die is gain. But if I live in the flesh, this is the fruit of my labor: yet what I shall choose I wot not. For I am in a strait betwixt two, having a desire to depart, and to be with Christ; which is far better"? Phil. i. 21–23. Eighteen centuries have rolled around since the apostle uttered that declaration. How many more years shall pass before the resurrection God only knows. Can any man suppose that the intensely energetic mind of Paul, used to action, and loving action, in the cause of his Redeemer, and ever on the wing from land to land in the advancement of the divine glory, would have esteemed it far better to sink into such a long period of unconsciousness and inactivity? Better to be in a condition in which for hundreds and hundreds of years he should know nothing, think nothing, feel nothing, than to enjoy those rapturous views of God and heaven which he had when caught up into Paradise? Better to be an inert, passive thing, doing nothing for Christ, enjoying nothing of Christ, than to be laboring continuously for the glory of God in the salvation of souls, and in that labor tasting the joy of the Lord as his strength? No, no! With all the spirits of the just made perfect he is now, and has been since he died, as active as he ever was in the body. His life had been one of intense sufferings—did ever any man have more of them?—but it was not merely relief from them that made death desirable. It was the assurance of being immediately with Jesus, and in the active enjoyment of his presence, that impelled the apostle to ecstasy.

It may be added that the parable of the rich man and Lazarus affords additional proof of this position. Activity is there, both in Abraham and Dives; and the time covered by the parable is the period between death and the resurrection, for the five brethren of the rich man were still living on the earth.

There is one passage in the Old Testament which forcibly expresses the fact that while the bodies are lying in the graves their souls continue active: "The righteous perisheth and no man layeth it to heart: and merciful men are taken away, none considering that the righteous is taken away from the evil. He shall enter into peace: they shall rest in their beds, each one walking in his uprightness." Isa. lvii. 1, 2. The word "walk" is in Scripture frequently used to express the whole active life. Thus, "walk worthy of the vocation wherewith ye are called" (Eph. iv. 1)—that is, live daily in such a manner as becomes your high position. So Isaiah declares that, while the bodies of the righteous rest in their graves as in their beds, the souls are living, acting, in their uprightness.

But what does the Bible mean when it speaks of death as a sleep? This is one of the most delightful images under which death is represented in the inspired volume. Thus, instead of saying that Stephen died, it is declared "he fell asleep." Acts vii. 60.

Notwithstanding the various passages of Scripture which have been quoted, some understand by this a cessation of all action, a passive, inactive state not only in the body, but in the soul as well. They suppose it is possible for the soul to be without the exercise of thought. This erroneous philosophy applied to revelation puts a false interpretation upon it; and it is one instance of the fact that the different interpretations, which prevail in the Church, of those passages of the word of God that draw their expressions from, or border on, human science are not the fault of the Bible itself, but of the erroneous impressions, and the erroneous systems of philosophy, which men bring with them to the book and place between their minds and the inspired words. But the only idea which we have of the soul is that it is a substance which thinks and feels and wills. If we conceive of it as losing its power to act, we divest it of all that we really know about it. We believe, however, that the soul never sleeps, never becomes unconscious and inactive for a single moment, even in this life. What we call sleep, what we need to enjoy every day, is the suspension of communication between the soul and the external world caused by the weary, worn-out condition of the body, or rather of the nervous system, which is the means of communication. Self-consciousness is lost—the *ego* as related to time and place and external circumstances. All the while the soul is thinking, but the means of communication with the outside world are suspended; the wires are down, the electric fluid does not pass over them, no message can be received from or sent to the world. That this is so appears from this consideration: Dreams belong to an imperfect sleep, or to a transition state between sound sleep and perfect waking. In that state the body, or the nervous part of it, is not entirely asleep. The thoughts of the mind pass over it, and we are conscious of them, in their connection with the external world, though in a disjointed or exaggerated form. The inference is strong that the mental activity is always going on; but in a very sound sleep, when the bodily senses are altogether locked up, or the nervous communication prostrated, we are not conscious of them, or do not remember them.

We are inclined to think, then, that this expression is, in the Bible, applied only to the body. A body that has just died and one that is asleep look very much alike. Therefore the same term is used for both conditions, though the cause of the appearance in each is different. This is all the word "sleep" itself suggests. It refers to the supine appearance of the body—its falling back and sinking down through the relaxation of the muscles. This is the first fact obvious to the eye as regards the sleeping body; and the same thing appears in a corpse.

This application is sustained by the declaration in the book of Daniel, where the expression is applied not only to the righteous, but also to the wicked: "Many of them that sleep in the dust of the earth shall awake, some to everlasting life, and some to shame and everlasting contempt." Dan. xii. 2, 3. That declaration, too, is directly limited to the body, for the soul does not sleep in the dust.

In this view the expression means that "dead bodies are destitute of sense and incapable of labor. They sleep in the dust free from pain and fatigue themselves, and incapable of being the means of affecting with weariness or suffering the spirit with which they were once so closely conjoined."* How delightful this is! And as we gaze upon the dead body of a Christian friend, how sweetly come the words:

"The languishing head is at rest,
Its thinking and aching are o'er;
The quiet, immovable breast
Is heaved by affliction no more.

"The heart is no longer the seat
Of trouble and torturing pain;
It ceases to flutter and beat,
It never will flutter again.

* "The Dead in Christ," by John Brown, D. D., p. 37.

"The lids which so seldom could close,
By sorrow forbidden to sleep,
Now, sealed in their mortal repose,
Have for ever forgotten to weep."

If, however, the souls of believers are to be brought within the application of the word, it means that "to them the state of death is a state free from peril. . . . There is no more hazard in death to a Christian than in sound sleep to a healthy man. Rather, it is like the salutary sleep which often terminates disease and restores to health. It is the peaceful interval between the distempered state of the present evil world and the absolutely perfect rest which is to follow the resurrection. . . . Freed from the evils of life, from the temptations of Satan, from the remains of sin, the departed saint is an entire stranger to fatigue and pain. He has desires, but no disquieting ones. His desires arise not from a painful sense of destitution, but entirely from the assurance of a still higher degree of holy happiness to meet enlarged capacities for it. He has hope, but it is unmingled with fear. It is the full, assured expectation of the adoption, the redemption of the body and of the glories and joys of the final state, the grace that is to be brought to him at the revelation of Jesus Christ." *

With this explanation we may adopt the beautifully musical verses which Tennyson wrote on the death of a very dear friend, and in which he unites soul and body as enjoying the sleep, though the verses are not exactly correct in point of theology or philosophy:

"Sleep sweetly, tender heart, in peace;
Sleep, holy spirit, blessed soul,
While the stars burn, the moons increase,
And the great ages onward roll.

"Sleep till the end, true soul and sweet,
Nothing comes to thee new or strange;
Sleep full of rest from head to feet;
Lie still, dry dust, secure of change."

* "The Dead in Christ," by John Brown, D. D., pp. 35–39.

Consider death, therefore, as the wonderful translation of the soul, with all its activities, from the land of conflict to the land of triumph. Look not at it with the glamour of a dead body on the eye. The physical frame, after a struggle with sickness and pain, falls over and is quiet; no action, no life, is in it. But the soul, almost ere the pulse has ceased to beat, at one bound, quicker than the lightning flash, we cannot doubt, mounts aloft to paradise. Unperceived by human eyes it passes away from the room in which the earthly tabernacle lies cold and stiff; but not so does it enter the building of God, the house not made with hands. It makes a glorious entrance into the new Jerusalem. Before we are certain that the breath has left the body the soul is crowned with an eternal crown from the hand of the Redeemer, and enthroned upon an everlasting throne; for the promises are: "Be thou faithful unto death, and I will give thee a crown of life;" and

"To him that overcometh will I grant to sit with me in my throne, even as I also overcame and am set down with my Father in his throne." Rev. ii. 10; iii. 21. Angels receive it. Spirits of the just made perfect who have gone before look on it with rapture, and welcome it to their number. And at once it takes its place among the innumerable multitude who worship the glorified Lamb, saying: "Thou wast slain, and hast redeemed us to God by thy blood out of every kindred, and tongue, and people, and nation: and hast made us unto our God kings and priests: and we shall reign on the earth." Rev. v. 9. It has life in its high spiritual form, without cessation, without alloy, pure and perfect in all its manifestations. This is the rich assurance which we have in reference to the present condition of our glorified redeemed. This is the precious hope with which, through a penitent faith in the crucified One, we approach our own death.

For his saved people Jesus has abolished death. Their bodies fall asleep in him, and rest in the bed which he has sanctified. Their souls are at once translated to paradise. In strict truth, therefore,

> "It is not death to die,
> To leave this weary road,
> And 'midst the brotherhood on high
> To be at home with God.
>
> "It is not death to close
> The eye long dimmed by tears,
> And wake in glorious repose
> To spend eternal years.
>
> "It is not death to bear
> The wrench that sets us free
> From dungeon chain to breathe the air
> Of boundless liberty.
>
> "It is not death to fling
> Aside this sinful dust,
> And rise on strong exulting wing
> To live among the just.
>
> "Jesus, thou Prince of life,
> Thy chosen cannot die;
> Like thee, they conquer in the strife,
> To reign with thee on high."

CHAPTER VI.

THE EMPLOYMENTS OF SOULS IN PARADISE.

AVING seen that souls continue active after they leave the body, it will be interesting to consider how they act.

On the general subject of their employment in Paradise the following remarks should be kept in mind:

1. From the activity of the soul, during the period between death and the resurrection, we ought to dissociate everything that is physical. We must not think of it as acting in any way through material organs, or in the modes in which it does here through the senses. Bodily movements, occupations and enjoyments must be rejected. Here lies one radical defect of

modern "spiritualism," so called, though it is really the baldest kind of materialism. It represents disembodied spirits as engaged in bodily works similar to those which occupied their attention on earth; a good old grandmother, for instance, as having knitting-needles in heaven and busily plying her vocation in a land where there are no cold feet to need stockings!

2. The native and the acquired sinless powers and capacities of the soul, so far at least as they are not dependent upon the bodily senses, are retained in active exercise. Two radical changes pass upon the saved human spirit at death—its perfect release from sin and its deliverance from the trammels of the body, with perhaps the development of powers which were not manifested while caged up in a cramping and sinful tabernacle. With the exception of these two sudden changes, "the life after death is an immediate continuation of the present life The soul is not altered in

death, but takes along with it its dispositions, its habits and whole tendency into the future world. The life to come taken in connection with the present make together one whole, even as manhood is only the continuation of youth." * "The laws of all the visible elements may vanish; the discoveries of science, as far as they are experimental discoveries, may yet be superseded by laws and relations of a different character, if a reason should exist to command the alteration; but, from the nature of the system to which he belongs, the principal laws of conscious being may be presumed to be interwoven in its permanent identity, and thence to be its laws for ever." †

It is but the application of this principle to say that sinless peculiarities of mind, which, in the kingdom of grace, mark different men, may be retained and continue

* Knapp's "Christian Theology," sec. cxlviii. 2.

William Archer Butler.

active in heaven, so that there will be a diversified active life there. If a man, under the influence of his home and collegiate education, has developed a philosophical, or a scientific, or a poetic, or a mathematical character, he does not, when he becomes converted to God, lose that character. Regeneration does not destroy it. Sanctification does not wear it away. The influence of the Spirit brings it, and its acquired treasures, and its active powers, into the service of Jesus. There is nothing irrational or unscriptural in the supposition that these differences, which men take into the kingdom of grace on earth, may accompany them into the kingdom of glory in heaven. Mental and moral habits which have been acquired by repeated practice, and carefully cultivated and employed for God, will not be cast behind as the soul enters the beautiful land. So far from this being the case, we may suppose, on the contrary, that they will find a larger scope for their exercise than they had here, and be used for ever to glorify God.

This is an important principle. We shall enter heaven with the sinless character which, under the influence of God's grace, we have formed here. So that every improvement that we make tells on eternity.

3. The activity of these powers of the soul is intensified in paradise. The life of heaven is a higher spiritual life than this. It is free from the limitations and imperfections of the body of sin. The soul on entering it must be quickened into wonderfully increased energy. It seems to be the teaching of Peter that the spirit of Jesus was thus quickened as it ascended from the cross; and if that could be the case with his pure spirit when liberated from his sinless body, much more must it be so in the case of the souls of the just which are released from imperfect and diseased bodies.

This is a delightful thought. There are many around us, some dear to us, who, through a defective bodily organization, show weak, inactive, sluggish minds. The soul looks very dimly out through the windows of sense upon the world. All of us have pains and defects which interfere with and cripple the mind in its action. Disease and trouble sadly mar our mental efforts. From all these we shall ere long be released; and the soul shall mount up to God rejoicing in its inherent energy, burning in reflected brightness before the throne, waiting for a glorified body like unto the glorified form of Jesus, which shall have no defect and be a meet temple for the soul through the remaining eternity.

4. The activity of the disembodied souls is uninterrupted. They need no repose or relaxation, for they "rest not day and night" (Rev. iv. 8) praising God. "They serve him day and night in his temple." Rev. vii. 15. While the alternations of day and night here bring along with them the necessity for rest, it is not so with the spirits of the

just in heaven. They never weary nor experience fatigue.

Their activity is, in a high sense, in the service of God. They ever worship him. Everything that is in them, every new discovery they make, gives them new food for praise. It is not true that the employment of heaven is "little more than a grand eternal act of worship by singing psalms of praise." This, it is to be feared, is the view that many have. They look upon heaven as an unspeakably happy place, in which they seem to imagine the redeemed will be doing nothing all the while but looking at Jesus and singing to him—that they will be so wrapped up in that as to be thinking of and doing nothing else, and so enraptured with the sight of Jesus as to desire to know no one else. This is a very incomplete view of the life of heaven. There is, however, a foundation for it in a superficial reading of the revelations of Scripture which make so much of worship. No doubt that is a chief employment of the beautiful land, "for praise is but the necessary expression of love, admiration, joy. In what way this praise is to be expressed I know not—whether in the spontaneous exercise of individual souls, 'singing as they shine,' with hymned voices and fashioned instruments of golden harp or angelic trumpet, or only by the rapid gaze of a spirit absorbed in still communion; and whether in heaven as on earth there may be great days of the Lord on which the sons of God, gathered from far, will come specially before the exalted Redeemer, when their joy, uttered by outbursts of harmony, shall awake the amphitheatre of the skies with impassioned hallelujahs, who can as yet tell?"* But praise in some form there is, and every new acquisition that the soul makes in knowledge and in activity gives a new sentiment to its song; every advance that it makes onward and upward in the perfect yet ever

* Norman McLeod's "Parish Papers," pp. 136, 137.

progressive life of heaven makes it thrill with another note; every new soul that joins the heavenly choir increases its sympathy and volume. With all the powers and all the knowledge that redeemed souls have when they enter heaven they commence the strain; and every communication that is made to them, every increase in knowledge, gives them fresh materials with which to magnify their God.

Under this thought we may group some of those mental powers which are specially represented in the Bible as engaged in the service. Let it be observed that the word of God does not profess to give full descriptions of heaven. Its great object is to teach us how to get there. The hints which it throws out, about the activity of its inhabitants and their mode of life, are only incidental and in connection with other things. We do not look upon them as complete. They leave much for us to find out when we reach the blessed land. What we exhibit now we cull as clusters of Engedi. From what is certainly given we can infer much more.

The memory of souls, while out of their bodies, is active. "Son, remember" (Luke xvi. 25), said Abraham to the rich man of the parable. This is involved also in the new song which is sung in heaven between death and the resurrection: "Thou art worthy to take the book, and to open the seals thereof; for thou wast slain and hast redeemed us to God by thy blood out of every kindred, and tongue, and people, and nation." Rev. v. 9. The glorified spirits of the just made perfect continue to have a vivid recollection of redemption's story, of their own winning to Christ, and of their conflicts in the spiritual life.

But they also receive further knowledge. Much of their own past history was an enigma while on earth. There is much that the Bible does not explain about the creation of this world, with which the geologist often tries to puzzle the humble child of God; much that is unknown in the past history of the world. There are many difficulties in the inspired book with which the acute skeptic may annoy us. All these, we doubt not, glorified souls have cleared up when they enter heaven, so that the least of them knows more than the mightiest scholar here.

It has been well remarked that a child who has read the first ten chapters of the book of Genesis is better instructed in ancient history than the greatest man of literature and speculation who has not the Bible in his hands. We feel assured that every soul that has passed into the new Jerusalem knows more about the secrets of the earth, its creation and its history, than all the schools of the world's geologists; more of the history of man and of the nations of the earth than all its historians; and more of science than all its natural philosophers.

Let this comfort the poor hard-working Christian who cannot get time to study the world's literature, but who is in his lowly place serving the Lord with the knowledge he has. As the Bible has infinitely more positive truth about man, his early existence and his destiny than all the speculations of philosophers, so the first ray that falls from the great white throne upon the soul as it enters heaven banishes much of the mystery that the Bible intentionally leaves over us here, and makes clear and precise what is now obscure and vague.

To guard, however, against an erroneous inference which some might draw from this —that, no matter how they live, if they are just saved at the last, they shall be equal in heaven to the greatest and most useful saints—it should be observed that in the glorified society "there can be no sameness either in the past history or in the intellectual capacity of its members. How vast must be the difference between the history of Gabriel, the thief on the cross, the apostle Paul and the child who died on its first birthday!"* Those who think that a death-bed repentance, if they can only make sure of that, or a sluggish Christian life, which selfishly presumes to rejoice in their own salvation while little or nothing is done for the advancement of Christ's glory in the salvation of others, will introduce them to heaven on a level with the zealous and active followers of Jesus, misapprehend the great doctrine of reward (of grace and for Christ's sake indeed, but) according to our works.

Further, new glories of creation burst upon glorified souls and are apprehended by their perceptive powers. It is of redeemed spirits before the resurrection of their bodies that John declares, in his apocalyptic vision, that they "fell down before him that sat on the throne, and worshiped him that liveth for ever and

* "Parish Papers," by Norman McLeod, D. D., p. 125.

ever, and cast their crowns before the throne saying, Thou art worthy, O Lord, to receive glory, and honor, and power: for thou hast created all things, and for thy pleasure they are and were created." Rev. iv. 10, 11. Do they simply have new views of past creations? or does their power of perception extend into new regions of infinitude where God's creative power is still being exercised? Do new worlds burst upon their view? and are they glorifying God for them? Is God ever creating? and are they ever beholding new works of his hand?

Moreover, the progress of Christ's kingdom on earth is made known to them as it advances. If there be joy in the presence of God among the angels and among the glorified redeemed over the repentance of souls, the knowledge of that repentance must, whenever it occurs, reach the blessed place. Every new destruction of Satan's power is also revealed to them; for we read again of the period before the resurrection: "I heard a loud voice saying in heaven, Now is come salvation and strength and the kingdom of our God and the power of his Christ; for the accuser of the brethren is cast down, which accused them before God day and night. And they overcame him by the blood of the Lamb and by the word of their testimony, and they loved not their lives unto the death. Therefore, rejoice, ye heavens, and ye that dwell in them." Rev. xii. 10–12.

How the disembodied souls obtain all this information we shall not seek to determine. We believe, though, they perpetually receive new and bright revelations from God, beginning in a peculiar manner at death:

"Putting off their mortal vesture, in their source their souls they steep;
Truth by actual vision learning, on its form their gaze they keep,
Drinking from the living fountains draughts of living waters deep."

They learn from Jesus, from the angels whose companions they are, from the redeemed who have gone before and with whom they associate; for they are with Abraham and Isaac and Jacob and all the glorified. For aught we can tell, also, the soul's powers of perception may be such that, even from the far-off place where heaven is, it can see this earth and pierce through creation's bonds. "Abraham sees the rich man in hell. The holy inhabitants of heaven see the smoke of the torment of the lost ascending up for ever and ever." May they not more easily perceive this earth and its passing transactions? Would not this give great point to the appeal of Paul: "Wherefore seeing we also are compassed about with so great a cloud of witnesses, let us lay aside every weight and the sin that doth so easily beset us"? Rev. xii. 1.

"The soul of man," says Dr. Archibald Alexander in his "Religious Experience," "though probably greatly enlarged in its powers, may have new faculties developed for which there was no use here and of which it had no consciousness; yet the field of knowledge being boundless, and our minds being capable of attaining only to one thing at a time, our knowledge of celestial things will be gradually acquired and not perfected at once," in the sense of possessing all that can be known, though what is known will be perfect in the sense of being accurate and free from error. The soul continues to learn when it enters heaven, and will go on learning for ever. "Indeed, there can be no limit set to the progress in knowledge, and it will be endless. No doubt the unalloyed pleasures of the future state will be intimately connected with this continual increase of divine knowledge. And as here knowledge is acquired by the aid of instructors, why may not the same be the fact in heaven? What a delightful employment to the saints, who have been drinking in the knowledge of God and his works for thousands of years, to communicate instruction to the saints just arrived! How delightful to conduct the pilgrim, who has just finished his race, through the ever-blooming bowers of paradise, and to introduce him to this and the other ancient believer, and to assist him to find out and recognize, among so great a multitude, old friends and earthly relatives!" * The recognition of friends in heaven is one source of the happiness of the blessed place, and the recognition is not confined to the bodily form. There is a recognition of souls.

Does it strike any humble-minded Christian with surprise to hear that as his soul at death enters heaven he may at once, after having gazed upon the glorified Jesus, meet some Old Testament saint whom he never saw in the flesh, or some dear Christian friends who had died before him, and that

* "Religious Experience," ch. xxii., p. 507; new edition.

they may tell him much about the glories of heaven, and take him to other saints and parted friends, and that with them he may hold communion about what has been passing on earth just before he left it? Shall he be surprised at the idea of the redeemed who had gone before telling him of what has taken place in heaven, and of his telling them what had just happened on earth? If so, is it not because heaven is not enough thought about as a social place with human souls in it?

At the transfiguration of Jesus, Moses and Elijah appeared communing with him of his decease. That transfiguration has ever been considered as a temporary appearance of the glory of heaven and of its life upon the earth. Thus Bishop Hall says in his "Meditations": "What comfort, what assurance of future blessedness, was thus afforded to those living witnesses who were present at this stupendous scene! With what joy did they behold these examples of the glory that shall be revealed! They saw in Moses and Elias what themselves should be after they had passed through the grave and gate of death." A desire to know about the future, then, and inquiries in regard to it, occupy glorified souls while out of the body.

Doubtless fields of active labor for Christ are found in paradise. Each soul does there the work for which it has been exquisitely adapted and carefully trained by the life of Christian discipline on earth. Heaven cannot be a world of listless inactivity, of holy idleness and mere rest, even with singing as an accompaniment. It must be "a world of action and unwearied diligence in doing God's will and in executing his commands." Otherwise it would be out of all analogy with the kingdom of grace, in which the first question put by the new-born soul is, "Lord, what wilt thou have me to do?" Acts ix. 6. It is a place of rest from the fatigue and weariness of labor, for

"Blessed are the dead which die in the Lord, yea, saith the Spirit, that they may rest from their labors, and their works do follow them" (Rev. xiv. 13); but it cannot be a place of cessation from holy labors which in a sinless state will bring no fatigue.

The various emotions and affections which flow from such knowledge and employments as have thus been referred to are involved in the activity of the soul—joy, gratitude, love to God and to the other redeemed, especially to those who were friends on earth, desire of knowledge, desire of society. The worship which the disembodied souls pay to God is one of rapturous gratitude in union and communion with each other, and this implies the ever-active exercise of all the powers of the soul. In the sixth chapter of the Revelation, John exhibits the souls of the martyrs as expressing a desire for justice upon the persecutors of the Church: "How long, O Lord, holy and true, dost thou not avenge our blood on them that dwell on the earth?" Rev. vi. 10.

If it be true that redeemed souls pass into the heavenly world with no sinless power or capacity destroyed, then, while we talk about them, they perceive, they remember, they converse with each other and with Christ, they reflect, they reason. They have no sorrow, no repentance, no remorse, no sinful feeling; but they have joy, and they sympathize in each other's joy; they enjoy the new and the wonderful, the beautiful and the sublime in nature which we now perceive, and much more which they perceive; they love each other; they enjoy each other's society; they desire to increase in knowledge; they worship God; they are instructed by the Redeemer directly and through other saints; and doubtless, since they are free from bodily trammels, mental powers are developed in them which in contrast leave us but as babblers in the divine life and in all knowledge.

Whether the glorified human spirits ever leave paradise to soar through other parts of the universe, or to make temporary visits to earth, the Bible does not say. We cannot deny the possibility of their returning here, and even of making revelations to living men, if such were the will of God. But there is nothing in the Bible to lead us to believe in such a return as an actual fact; and most certainly new revelations are not made to men on earth through their instrumentality. They are ever learning much that is new; but the Bible contains all the revelation that God has designed to make to us while we are here. This is our all-sufficient guide for this life. The canon is closed: "If any man shall add unto these things, God shall add unto him the plagues that are written in this book." Rev. xxii. 18.

As to the activity of glorified saints and angels, such a cautious and scriptural writer as Dr. Archibald Alexander wrote in his "Religious Experience": "It need not be supposed that saints in heaven will be continually employed in nothing but praise. This, indeed, will be their noblest employment, and the anthems of praise to God and the Lamb will never cease; but may we not reasonably suppose that the exercises and pursuits of the saints will be various? The wonderful works of God will open to their contemplation. They may be employed as angels are now, as messengers to distant worlds, either as instruments of justice or mercy, for we find that the angels are employed in both these ways. While, then, one choir surrounds the throne and elevates the celestial song of praise for redemption, others may be employed in executing the commands of their Lord; and then, in their turn, these last may keep up the unceasing praise, while the first go forth on errands of mercy or wrath."*

Hence all Christian training here will be of use there. "Can it be," says Dr. Nor-

* "Religious Experience," pp. 513, 514, new edition.

man McLeod, "that our moral habits and Christian graces shall never be called into exercise in works and labors of love among orders of beings of whom as yet we know nothing? Countless worlds may be teeming with immense populations; and who knows but such worlds may be continually added to the great family of God? And if throughout the endless ages of eternity, or in any province of God's boundless empire, there should ever be found some responsible beings who are tempted to depart from God by the machinations of wicked men or evil spirits—permitted then, it may be, as well as now, to use all their powers in the service of sin and against the kingdom of God—and who, being thus tempted, shall require warning or support to retain them in their allegiance; or if there be found others who are struggling in an existence which, however glorious, demands patience, fortitude and faith in Jehovah; if there are now in other worlds, or ever shall appear, any persons who need such ministrations as can be afforded only by those educated in the wonderful school of Christ's Church,—then can I imagine how God's saints from earth may have glorious labors given them throughout eternity which they alone, of all the creatures of God, will be able to accomplish, when every holy habit acquired here can be put to noble uses there. I can conceive patience needed to overcome difficulties, and faith to trust the living God amidst evolutions of his providence that baffle the understanding; and indomitable courage, untiring zeal, gentle love, heavenly serenity and intense sympathy, yea, even the peculiar gifts and characteristics of each individual, all having their appropriate and fitting work given them. 'Now *abideth* faith, hope, charity; but the greatest of these is charity.' And what immense joy will be experienced in each saint thus finding an outlet for his love, and exercise for his knowledge, and full play for his every faculty, in that house of many mansions, with all God's universe around and eternity before him!

"Let this comfort us when we see 'such a one as Paul the aged' fall asleep after his day of toil, and strengthen us to bow our heads in meekness when we hear of the young man full of zeal and ardor, apparently fully equipped for God's service, suddenly cut down, or the self-sacrificing missionary who seems to have spent his strength in vain perish with no one in the wilderness to give him a burial. Oh, think not that the work of the old saint, who loved it so well till the last hour of his existence, is ended for ever, or that the labors of younger brethren, so unfinished here, shall never be resumed hereafter, and that all this preparation of years has been a mere abortion, a mockery and delusion. Believe it not. No day of conscientious study for Christ's sake has been spent in vain, no habit of industry or self-denial acquired for Christ's sake has been acquired in vain, nor will the burning zeal to do something for Him who died for them be ever lost in darkness or put to shame. Soul, spirit and body will yet do their work for which they have been so exquisitely adapted and so carefully trained." *

* "Parish Papers," pp. 134–136.

CHAPTER VII.

THE HOLINESS AND HAPPINESS OF SOULS IN PARADISE.

REDEEMED souls enter paradise perfectly holy. The Holy Spirit completes his sanctifying work at death. Old things then utterly and for ever pass away from the regenerate spirit, and all things become entirely new. All the remains of corruption and of inclinations to sin are rooted out of it; and in that holiness the departed souls are confirmed. They can never more sin; they are not exposed to temptation; they are "the spirits of the just made perfect" (Heb. xii. 23); they are "without fault before the throne of God." Rev. xiv. 5. There shall in no wise enter into heaven anything that defileth, neither whatsoever worketh abomination or maketh a lie. Glorious state! No sin! No temptation! No corrupt will! No unholy inclinations! No evil dispositions! No serpent among the trees of the heavenly paradise! All like Christ! Delightful termination of a long conflict which is waged here, not against flesh and blood, but against principalities and powers!

It is not death that effects this change, though it pleases God to accomplish it then. There is something wonderful about it. If Nicodemus was startled when Jesus declared the mystery of the new birth, this is quite as astonishing. The human mind can scarcely grasp the wonderful extent of the transformation which is wrought in that moment of time. For reach whatever standard of holiness the believer may in this world, while there is the slightest taint of sin in him, he is at an infinite remove from the likeness of the all holy One. "To many it is the subject of distressing perplexity that persons of unquestioned piety sometimes continue to manifest great imperfections to the very end of their life. Even at the near approach of their transition from the earthly state to the heavenly their sanctification seems to be immature. The mind of Dr. Guthrie appears to have been strongly impressed by this enigma in Christian experience, of which he could offer no other solution than that a change must take place at the moment of death second only to that at the moment of conversion. 'There is much sin to be cast off,' he says, 'like a slough, with this mortal flesh. Saw we the spirit at its departure, as Elisha saw his ascending master, we might see a mantle of imperfection and infirmity dropped from the chariot that bears it in triumph to the skies. I have thought that there must be a mysterious work done by the Spirit of God in the very hour of death to form the glorious crown and cope-stone of all his other labors, and that, like the wondrous but lovely plant which blows at midnight, grace comes out in its perfect beauty amid the darkness of the dying hour. How that is done I do not know. It takes one whole summer to ripen the fields of corn and five hundred years to bring the oak to its full maturity; but He at whose almighty word this earth sprang at once into perfect being, loaded with orchards and golden harvests and clustering vines and stately palms and giant cedars, man in ripened manhood and woman in her full-blown charms, is able in the twinkling of an eye, ere our fingers have closed the filmy orbs or we have stooped to print our last fond kiss on the marble brow, to crown the work his grace begun. With him one day is as a thousand years. He shall perfect that which concerneth you. He shall bring forth the head-stone thereof with shouting, crying, Grace, grace unto it.' "*

* "Man, Moral and Physical," by the Rev. Joseph H. Jones, D. D., p. 277.

The perfect holiness of the disembodied spirits of the redeemed is inseparably connected with their perfect happiness, to which, therefore, we proceed. On this it should be remarked:

1. That their happiness is perfect, but not complete, between the death and resurrection of their bodies. Every capacity that they have in themselves for pleasure is perfectly satisfied, but still they look forward to something higher. They have joys of anticipation as well as of memory and action. "The separation of the body from the soul is not in itself desirable. It is the consequence of a derangement of the original state of things, which, when God contemplated it after he had established it, appeared to his all-perfect, infinitely holy, wise and benignant mind very good. God made man immortal, and formed him an image of his own eternity. Death entered by sin. It is a penal evil, an expression of the displeasure of God at the violation of the primitive constitution

under which man was placed."* "The fact of the resurrection proves that with man at least the state of a disembodied spirit is a state of unnatural violence, and that the resurrection of the body is an essential step to the highest perfection of which he is susceptible."

The happiness of the soul in paradise is higher, far higher, than the happiness of our present life. Elements of joy it has which we have not now. But it is not as high as will be the happiness of the resurrection state. Therefore our Larger Catechism says that while the souls of the redeemed are at death "made perfect in holiness and received into the highest heavens, where they behold the face of God in light and glory," they are "waiting for the full redemption of their bodies, which even in death continue united to Christ and rest in their graves as in their beds, until at the last day they be again united to their

* "The Dead in Christ," by John Brown, D. D., p. 41.

souls." Ques. 86. They lose not the recollection of their earthly tenements. They wait for the sinless reconstruction of them. Those bodies in their graves are mingled with the bodies of the wicked, for the complete separation from which the souls wait and look forward with ardent desire. The calling up of the body from the grave and its reconstruction like unto the glorious body of Jesus, and the dwelling in and activity of the soul through that bright and shining form; the transactions of the public judgment day; the approval of the believer before the universe in connection with the vindication of all God's ways; the public utterance of the invitation, "Come unto me;" and the re-entrance of soul and body united into the everlasting joy of the Lord,—shall consummate and make complete the perfect happiness which begins to be experienced at death.

2. The happiness of all glorified souls is perfect, but not equal. Neither the inter-

mediate nor the final state is one in which all the saved have an equal measure of bliss. They enter heaven with great differences between them. "Blessed are the dead which die in the Lord, from henceforth; yea, saith the Spirit, that they may rest from their labors, and their works do follow them." Rev. xiv. 13. Their works do follow them when they die. We conceive of two ways in which our works will follow us into heaven. We shall take along with us the remembrance of them, and we shall meet with their happy results. If, under the grace of Christ, we have brought other souls to salvation or helped them on in their course, we shall meet with the fruits of our works in knowing that those souls have been saved, recognizing them in heaven, and while recognizing them remembering the good which we did to them for the sake of our one Redeemer.

Compare, then, in their death, the penitent malefactor who was saved from the cross and the apostle Paul. The sinner saved from the jaws of death went up from the cross to heaven with the prayer quivering from the lips, "Lord, remember me when thou comest into thy kingdom." How great was his joy as he passed through the pearly gate to know that he was saved for ever! But all that he could remember with any pleasure was that simple act of faith. No good works done through grace could follow him on which he could look with pleasure. He was happy, perfectly happy, according to his capacity. His gush of bliss in ascending from the cross of a thief to the crown of a king, saved by grace, was unutterable, and he could magnify the mercy of God in a strain which would attract the admiring attention of all heaven. But the apostle Paul entered the glorious land with these triumphant words: "I have fought a good fight; I have finished my course; henceforth there is laid up for me a crown of righteousness." 2 Tim. iv. 7. His memory was charged with years of activity and holy zeal spent in the service of his dear Redeemer. They were so inwrought with the texture of his soul that they could not be torn from it without its destruction. Souls were waiting for him whom he had been the instrument, through his preaching and his self-denying work, of leading to the cross. To this day soul after soul is entering heaven saved through his writings. In his own mind and in the society of heaven he has had, and ever shall have, springs of joy which the eleventh-hour convert cannot have.

"The more difficulties the saints have passed through in their way to heaven, the place will be the sweeter to them when they come at it. Every happy stroke struck in the spiritual warfare will be a jewel in their crown of glory. Each victory obtained against sin, Satan and the world will raise their triumphant joy the higher. The remembrance of the cross will sweeten the crown, and the memory of their travel through the wilderness will put additional verdure on the fields of glory while they walk through them minding the day when they went mourning without the sun." *

3. The happiness of each redeemed soul is perfect when it enters paradise, but it is not stationary. It is an ever-increasing bliss. Increasing knowledge and increasing activity bring along with them increasing capacities and sources of enjoyment. The more the redeemed learn of the works and ways of God—and this they will ever be doing—the more and the deeper will be the fountains of their enjoyment. In the singularly expressive words of one of the Middle Age hymn-writers,

"Ever filled and ever seeking, what they have they still desire;
Hunger there shall fret them never, nor satiety shall tire;
Still enjoying whilst aspiring, in their joy they still aspire."

In forming our views of the various elements which constitute the happiness of

* Boston's "Fourfold State," p. 309.

paradise, it should be remembered that whatever true spiritual enjoyment any soul has here is continued in it, and that additional pleasures flow from the continued exercise of all those mental powers which continue active. Here the word paradise, expressing a place of peculiar joy, applied to the heavenly home, is very suggestive. It carries us back to man's happiness before the fall. The great idea conveyed by it is that of a restoration to a condition the same in kind with that in which man was created, though higher in degree, and doubtless with added elements of joy, because of the union of God with human nature and the blessings purchased by redemption through which men are advanced above the angels.

"Sin is a perversion of human nature, not its annihilation—a disorder of its powers, not their destruction. Nor is restoration by Jesus Christ the gift of a different constitution, as if he made us something else than human beings, but the renovation of the old constitution after its original type. . . . That which would constitute the happiness of man, were he perfect on earth, will be his happiness, though in a higher degree, when he is made perfect in heaven. This supposition only assumes the fact that we shall be the same persons for ever, that human nature will never cease to be human nature, or be changed into a different species of existence, no more than Jesus Christ, the head of his Church, will ever cease to be what he is, the man Christ Jesus with a human body and a human soul, the same yesterday, to-day and for ever."*

But we shall particularly mention the elements in the happiness of the soul's intermediate state which none of us have here. These are in addition to the spiritual joys of this life.

1. The glorified souls are freed from all positive evil. How much is embraced in

* "Parish Papers," by Norman McLeod, D. D., p. 98, 99.

this statement—perfect freedom from all sin and from all suffering! This bliss alone would be ecstatic. Notice some of the things that are included in it:

(1.) Perfect deliverance from sin. Can any one imagine the thrill of joy which must pass over a soul at the instant of death as it flies from the body heavenward, with the delightful assurance that all sin is for ever left behind? It has something of the unalloyed happiness of the holy God. The hour when first it believed in Jesus is a precious one in memory, but can it be compared with that? Paul once cried out, even after he had made great progress in holiness, "O wretched man that I am, who shall deliver me from the body of this death?" Rom. vii. 24. When his glorified Lord summoned him from earth his soul was quickly borne aloft by angels, while in ecstasy he was able to exclaim, Blessed Redeemer, thou hast now delivered me! And so the joy of perfect holiness belongs to every saved soul immediately on its translation from the body.

(2.) Freedom from all suffering caused by bodily disease and deprivations. So intimate is the union between soul and body that the imperfections and the pains of the latter must sadly affect the former. The religious exercises of the soul are often interfered with, its communion with God is marred, by bodily weaknesses and pains. But the disembodied spirits are free from all this. They "rest from their labors." Rev. xiv. 13. Spiritual exercises are no longer a weariness. The glorified never faint, never become tired in them.

(3.) Freedom from the dread of dying. Notwithstanding our victory through Christ, there continues to be a sting in death. Even the believer shrinks from the pain, and the sufferings, and the breakings up connected with it. But in paradise mortality is swallowed up of life. The soul, ever fresh, ever young, rejoices in the blissful assurance that the hour of bodily death has passed, and that, instead of having to look forward to such an event, it awaits the hour of bodily reconstruction. In the song of redeemed souls before the resurrection Paul's triumphant exclamation must occupy a prominent place: "O death, where is thy sting? O grave, where is thy victory? The sting of death is sin, and the strength of sin is the law. But thanks be to God, which giveth us the victory through our Lord Jesus Christ." 1 Cor. xv. 55–57.

(4.) Freedom from the dread of falling any more into sin. No evil principle within, no temptation without, the blessed souls are not in constant need of watchfulness and prayer lest they fall. The crowns of triumph are on them. The rewards of victors have been bestowed upon them. No longer warriors engaged in the heat and dust of the conflict,

> "They walk the heavenly street,
> And ground their arms at Jesus' feet."

(5.) Perfect and everlasting separation from sinners. The glorified souls are no longer called upon to endure the taunts and the misrepresentations of the wicked, nor to mourn their close proximity to, and contact with, sin in its vilest forms. Sin and sinners alike are far away below the confines of the beautiful land, and unable to cause the first pang of grief in holy souls.

We know experimentally nothing of these blessings here. No man enjoys them in this world. There is no spot on earth where they can be found. No mere human heart this side the grave has ever tasted them. But there they are, just beyond the Jordan, in the beautiful land. Our glorified Christian friends have them now in perfection.

2. Another great source of happiness for the spirits of the just made perfect is found in their simple presence in the home of Jesus. They are with the Lord "In my

Father's house are many mansions. I go to prepare a place for you. And if I go and prepare a place for you, I will come again and receive you unto myself; that where I am, there ye may be also." John xiv. 1–4. And a place of great beauty that is. The paradise that was was exceeding fair. The paradise that is "is the holiest and happiest region of the universe, bearing some proportion in its superiority to Eden to that which the second man, the Lord from heaven, bears to the first man, who was of the earth, earthy." Here the soul, as it looks out through the narrow avenue of the bodily eye, derives an intense satisfaction from the contemplation of the beauties of nature; there, we cannot doubt, the glorified spirits are able to expatiate over scenes of beauty and of grandeur such as have never yet fallen upon our vision.

3. But the most glorious and the most beautiful object that they behold is Jesus

himself, with whom they are. The Lamb which is in the midst of the throne leads them to living fountains of water. This expresses nearness of approach by him to them. John saw him in the apocalyptic vision. The saved souls worship him. How they see him we cannot tell. It is not through bodily eyes. They have some other power of perception. Not only are they permitted to dwell in Jerusalem; they see the King's face. And the joy of that sight! We would like to have beheld Jesus of Nazareth while he was on the earth. We earnestly desire now to look upon him in his glorified body. We want to gaze upon that form whose head and whose hairs are white like wool, as white as snow, and his eyes as a flame of fire, and his feet as fine brass, as if they burned in a furnace; and to hear that voice which is as the sound of many waters; and to bask in the light of that countenance which is as the sun shineth in his strength We know that if we were to see and hear him now the vision would kill us, unsanctified that we are. But if it should be our privilege, completely changed by the Spirit of God, to enter the pearly gate, to gaze upon him would be almost happiness enough. The redeemed who have gone home to God have that blessedness now. "They burn with seraphic love, like coals of juniper, and the arch of heaven rings with their songs of salvation to Him that sitteth upon the throne and to the Lamb."

O Jesus! thy sweet memory
Can fill the heart with ecstasy;
But passing all things sweet that be,
  Thine actual presence, Lord.

4. But closer still: they not only look upon, they have habitual communion with, the glorified Redeemer. Nothing clouds or distracts or interferes with it. They are ever with the Lord; the Lord is ever with them. Seeing him as he is, they rest not day nor night praising him. The commu-

nion is enjoyed, not through ordinances, but directly; no longer a communion of faith, but one of sight; no longer of hope, at times clouded and dimmed, but of full yet increasing fruition. They have entered into the joy of their Lord. From the sacramental table of earth they have gone up to the richer feast of heaven. Nothing can ever come between them and Jesus. In his work the body here may wear out; there, they need never to rest from their spiritual services and communion.

5. Communion with other redeemed spirits is another source of happiness in paradise. We know not how it is carried on. We cannot tell how the separate souls communicate to each other and to God their thoughts and feelings. But the fact is plain. The glorified souls retain their social nature; and how widely extended is their communion! It includes the wise and good of all ages. What a joy to be permitted to converse with Abel, and Moses,

and Samuel, and David, and Isaiah, and John, and Peter, and Paul! It specially embraces friends who had preceded them to the happy land. Oh the heavenly joy of recognizing earth's purest friendships over again! "I trust to come unto you and speak face to face, that our joy might be full" (2 John 14), wrote the beloved apostle to some of his dear Christian friends. Perhaps his wish was not gratified on earth; but their souls have met in heaven. And so, if we go there, we shall find those who have crossed the Jordan before us, and shall live over again holy friendships, though divested of earth's carnal forms.

6. The society of angels is still another source of joy to the spirits of the just made perfect. Here the angels are ministering spirits sent forth to minister to the heirs of salvation, but between the two orders of creatures there is no joyous communion. In paradise, however, the Bible represents

them as mingling intimately among each other and joining in the same worship. "It has been finely said one angel's history may be a volume of more precious truth than all the records of our race." Volume after volume of such truth the glorified redeemed are permitted to scan.

"Oh how beautiful that region,
And how fair that heavenly legion,
Where those men and angels blend!
Glorious will that city be,
Full of deep tranquillity,
Light and peace from end to end!
All the happy dwellers there
Shine in robes of purity;
Keep the law of charity,
Bound in firmest unity.
Labor finds them not, nor care;
Ignorance can ne'er perplex,
Nothing tempt them,.nothing vex;
Joy and health their fadeless blessing,
Always all good things possessing."

CHAPTER VIII.

THE MANSIONS AND HOME LIFE OF PARADISE.

NE topic remains which blends especially with the employments and the happiness of souls in paradise. But it also brings together and condenses in a winning form the substance of all that has been presented. We, therefore, throw it into a separate chapter.

Our Redeemer, a few hours before his crucifixion, said to his sorrowing apostles, "In my Father's house are many mansions: if it were not so I would have told you. I go to prepare a place for you. And if I go and prepare a place for you, I will come again, and receive you unto myself; that where I am there ye may be also." John xiv. 2, 3.

A house; a father's house; the house of our Redeemer's Father; mansions in that house; and a place prepared there for us: how suggestive these expressions are of home life!

The Father's house is heaven. We have seen that it is a particular place now existing in the universe. It is far away from earth; but were our eyes keen enough, and spiritual enough, we might see,

> "Like the edges of a sunset cloud,
> The beatific land before us lie."

The Psalmist calls it "the place of God's habitation." Ps. xxxiii. 14.

The prophet Isaiah (lxiii. 15) designates it as the "habitation of God's holiness and glory."

It is the holy home of the universe, where the glory of God is especially witnessed, and his society intimately enjoyed. Not the whole universe itself, as some would suppose, with its different planets and stars, as the mansions spoken of; but a central place in that wide and illimitable universe.

Our Lord also once called the temple at Jerusalem his Father's house. John ii. 16.

That temple was the building in which God was especially represented to the Old Testament Church. Within it was the holy of holies, which, as we have seen, was in a pre-eminent manner a type of heaven. Hence our Saviour might well apply the same title to both places.

Round about and within that temple were chambers in which abode the priests who ministered in the religious services of the place. 1 Kings vi. 5–10. That, we suppose, suggested to the Redeemer his expression that there were many mansions, or "abiding-places," in the heavenly house which the earthly shadowed forth.

At first sight it would seem incongruous to speak of many mansions in one house; but when it is remembered that in the temple, which was one house, there were those separate abiding-places, the striking beauty of the expression at once appears.

Heaven is represented by it under the similitude of a temple containing rooms for all the members of the royal priesthood. God's redeemed people are kings and priests unto him. In his home there are everlasting abiding-places from which they go forth to its public services, and to which, from those services, they return for meditation and social communion with each other and with their Lord. Speaking with diffidence, and not intending to be as didactically positive as on points where revelation is fuller and more varied, this seems to be the Redeemer's meaning.

As has already been seen, this is not the only form in which heaven is pictured to us. Figures that, on the plane of earth, would really exclude each other, are blended in the Bible delineations in order to exhibit the multiform characteristics of the place. Thus it is

"A city, or a temple, or a home,
Or rather all in one."

It is so rich, so infinitely above any and all the things of earth, that no one description can embody its fullness. A home in its social character, a temple in its aspect of worship, a garden in its variety of delights, through the scriptural dissolving views it brightens and enlarges into a city in its size and the innumerable multitude of its inhabitants.

As heaven itself is a really existing place, a particular locality, we may suppose that the mansions spoken of by our Lord are real and circumscribed abodes in it. It seems to us that no other idea can fully bring out what may be called the topographical promises of the Bible.

"Make to yourselves friends of the mammon of unrighteousness," says our Lord, "that when ye fail they may receive you into everlasting *habitations.*" Luke xvi. 9.

Through his strong faith the apostle Paul

was able to say, "We know that if our earthly house of this tabernacle were dissolved, we have a building of God, an house not made with hands, eternal in the heavens." 2 Cor. v. 1. There are some who entertain the erroneous notion that the soul cannot act without a material body; that it depends on its union with an organism—at least for its intelligent connection with external things and with time.* Therefore,

* The more recent and least unscientific form which this assumes, opposing on the one hand the materialistic heresy that "life is the result of living matter, or one of its properties," but, on the other hand, erroneously making too much of our present experience, has thus been presented: "The more philosophical view as to the nature of the connection between life and its material basis is the one which regards vitality as something superadded and foreign to the matter by which vital phenomena are manifested. Protoplasm is essential as the physical medium through which vital action may be manifested; just as a conductor is essential to the manifestation of electric phenomena, or just as a paint-brush and colors are essential to the artist. Because metal conducts the electric current and renders it perceptible to our senses, no one thinks of therefore asserting that electricity is one of the inherent properties of a metal, any more than one would feel inclined to assert that the power of painting was inherent in the camel's hair or in the dead pigments. Be-

they think we are shut up to the conclusion either that at death the soul ceases to be active—at least with externally perceptive powers—or that it is immediately provided

hind the material substratum, in all cases, is the active and living force; and we have no right to assume that the force ceases to exist when its physical basis is removed, though it is no longer perceptible to our senses. It is, on the contrary, quite conceivable theoretically that the vital forces of an organism should suffer no change by the destruction of the physical basis, just as electricity would continue to subsist in a world composed universally of non-conductors. In neither case could the force manifest its presence, or be brought into any perceptible relation with the outer world; but in neither case should we have the smallest ground for assuming that the power was necessarily non-extant." (Dr. H. Alleyne Nicholson's "Introduction to the Study of Biology," p. 11.) "Electricity," however, "may be a force in nature manifested to us, in our present state, only under certain conditions. But that does not prove that it is active only under those conditions, or that beings constituted differently from what we are may not be cognizant of its activity." (Dr. Charles Hodge's "Systematic Theology," iii. 714.) And especially as to the soul, if, as the Bible teaches, it be a substance, and a different substance from the body, though receiving the latter into union with it as the human person, "it has power—power of self-manifestation, and productive power according to its nature." And it is certainly unscientific to say that, because in this stage of our existence it exerts and manifests its power in and through a body, it can only do it in that way.

with another body. And as it is plain that the apostle, in the passage we have quoted, is describing the period immediately after death, they adopt the latter inference. But it is very unphilosophical to declare that, because in this state of our existence our souls manifest their activity in connection with bodies in which they dwell, it must always be so. God, the great Spirit who is ever active, has no body. On the other hand, there is no intimation anywhere in the Bible of any bodies other than those which we now wear, and which shall be reconstructed as spiritual bodies at the last day. The apostle's declaration, therefore, was that at death his soul would immediately pass into heaven; and we see not why we should be content with the vague notion that the "building," the "house," was "heaven" itself, and not "*in* the heavens." He seems to assert that there was in heaven a "building," a divinely-made "house," a distinct "mansion" for his soul.

Of course we do not conceive of those mansions as anything like the brick-and-mortar dwellings or the marble palaces of earth. We are inclined, however, to suppose they are real and circumscribed places of abode for souls, and "counterparts for their spiritual characteristics."

It has been seen that the predominant character under which the Bible represents the life of heaven is that of praise. The inhabitants of the blessed land appear in magnificent choirs, harping upon their harps to the glory of the Most High. They rest not day nor night from this service. Worship never ceases in the heavenly temple. Never is the place silent. Always some of its inhabitants are engaged in praise.

But the glorious temple may have its grand convocation seasons. As it is written in the book of Job that there was a day when the sons of God came to present themselves before the Lord, so there may be seasons when, in a way which is possible for pure spirits, though inconceivable by us, the whole redeemed and angelic hosts may make the universe thrill with a mighty volume of praise, that rolls out from their home through stars and planets and worlds, to the infinite glory of their God—seasons imaged forth to us in the fifth chapter of the Revelation, where, before the Lamb in the midst of the throne, redeemed sinners with harps, and golden vials full of odors, sung the new song, Thou wast slain, and hast redeemed us to God by thy blood; and ten thousand times ten thousand and thousands of thousands of angels followed with a loud voice, saying, Worthy is the Lamb that was slain; to whom succeeded the whole intelligent creation, saying, Blessing, and honor, and glory, and power be unto him that sitteth upon the throne and unto the Lamb for ever and ever; after which the redeemed sinners closed the song in humblest prostration, saying, Amen! Amen!

Nor have we any doubt that, in addition to these public services of praise, there are many active employments in paradise for the redeemed. We hesitate not to believe that every native or acquired sinless habit of the soul, every developed capacity and cultivated power here used in the Redeemer's service, which sometimes the soul, taken away in early life, never employed fully on earth, finds a field for exercise in the heavenly world. The spiritual and active life of this world is a training-school for the land beyond the Jordan.

But it does not seem irrational or unscriptural to suppose that there are periods when the redeemed withdraw from that public praise, and from those public employments, to their own mansions for holy purposes similar to those which mark the spiritual social life of this lower world.

Those mansions speak to us of seasons of "calm, unbroken solitude for lonely meditation." From the scenes of surpassing glory, and from the public services of unutterable joy, that crowd heaven, the redeemed need places of retirement where they may gather and compose their thoughts in meditation, and receive the full benefit of their public outgoings.

They point us also to the domestic communion of friends in each other's mansions. For the sanctified friendships of earth, divested of their carnal relationships, renew themselves in paradise, and new friendships are formed. Love cannot be

> "Without the chosen specialties of love,
> The nearest to the nearest most akin."

The redeemed friends of earth and new friends of heaven mingle with each other in their abiding-places.

More delightful still, the Redeemer's comforting words whisper to us of home visits from the Lord himself, of times when the glorified humanity of Christ comes specially near and communes with each soul as friend with friend. When he was on earth, he was often found beneath the roof of the little family of Bethany, in friendly communings with its members. He is the same Jesus still. It is precisely this which was the great comfort of his words as they were addressed to his apostles. They had been, and were then, enjoying direct and personal communion with him. After his death and ascension, and until their death, they should be deprived of that bliss. But it would be restored to them. And surely that element of their happiness will be granted to all the saved. All Christians have a longing desire to see their Redeemer. The desire shall be gratified; not here, but above. And not merely do the glorified redeemed gaze from a distance upon him as "the enthroned monarch of the whole infinity of being;" it must be their privilege to be at times as near to him as the two disciples were during their walk to Emmaus on the evening of his resurrection—as our first parents were when he came down to visit them in the innocency of the first paradise.

The joy and the glory of those mansions, the endless capabilities of their mutual influence for happiness, are increased by their innumerable multitude. There are "*many*" of them. In the earthly temple the number of chambers for the priests was very small; in the heavenly, the abiding-places of redeemed souls cannot be counted by man.*

Moreover, the happiness of the blessed place is diversified by the differences which exist in glory, in brilliancy, in degree of dignity, among the mansions.

All saved souls enter heaven perfectly holy and happy. But in other respects—in their knowledge, in the treasures of

* We do not know on what authority Longfellow has presented heaven under the description of "a great cloister's stillness and seclusion." Certainly, it is not based upon the Bible. The place is large. Already it has multitudes of inhabitants. It will be crowded. Instead of a secluded and still life, the Bible represents it as for ever vocal with praise, and its denizens as actively engaged with each other and for God.

their memories, in their cultivated habits of usefulness—there must be as great a variety among them as exists here; and if their mansions be counterparts for their spiritual characteristics, the same variety may exist among those mansions.

The angels have their mansions different from those which belong to redeemed sinners; redeemed infants different from the aged saints; lifelong laborers in the Master's cause different from eleventh hour penitents.

All are indeed glorious. But the starry heavens, with their bright worlds of light, are glorious. Yet "there is one glory of the sun, and another glory of the moon, and another glory of the stars; for one star differeth from another star in glory." 1 Cor. xv. 41. So also may it be with the inhabitants of the Father's house, and with their mansions in it.

Degrees in heaven? Yes! Degrees of capacity to enjoy, while all are perfectly satisfied according to their capacity. Degrees of brilllancy with which the light that beams from the countenance of the King is reflected. Degrees of nearness to his throne. Degrees, therefore, in the splendor of the mansion in which the redeemed abide.

Whose mansions are the most glorious?

Not necessarily that of the rich saint who on earth dwelt in a magnificent house, richly furnished and munificently adorned with works of art. All the wealth of "Ormus and of Ind" cannot buy the heavenly splendor.

Not necessarily that of the man of power who, from his kingly or presidential palace, issued the orders which swayed the affairs of millions. Earth's imperial words have no influence over heaven's court—not as much as the pauper's trembling breath of faith.

Not necessarily that of the learned man who, from his splendid intellectual stores, fed his own mind and in turn nourished the craving minds of his fellows. The wisdom of earth cannot provide a key wherewith to open a celestial mansion.

All earthly things, when not accompanied by true piety, go for nothing in the kingdom of heaven. They help nothing in the glory of the Father's house unless they are subsidized to the service of the Lord.

But says the Redeemer, "Whosoever shall do and teach my commandments, the same shall be called great in the kingdom of heaven." Matt. v. 11.

Many a poor man shall have a more glorious mansion than his rich neighbor; many an ignorant man, as to the learning of the earth, a more shining position than the splendid intellect; many a woman unknown to the world, but laboring for Jesus, a more brilliant standing than any of earth's queens.

Zealous lives of faith, and love, and service for the Lord,—these graduate the heavenly scale. They that do most, according to their opportunities, for the salvation of other souls, are nearest to Him who came from the throne to save the lost. They that are most like him in spirit, in life, and in labors here, shall shine the most resplendently in his court through eternity.

"They that be wise shall shine as the brightness of the firmament: and they that turn many to righteousness as the stars for ever and ever." Dan. xii. 3.

Our crucified Lord ascended to heaven to prepare their mansions for his people: "I go to prepare a place for you."

The whole extent of his work of preparation there and now, in addition to his presentation as our advocate, we know not. The number of the mansions has been determined from eternity. But who can positively declare that some perpetual creative work of the Redeemer is not going on, by which he prepares for each soul its special mansion?

There is also a preparation-work in his people themselves for their mansions; and when that is finished, he comes to each of them in turn and takes them to their home. "If I go and prepare a place for you, I will come again and receive you unto myself, that where I am there ye may be also."

He comes to his redeemed by his Spirit in the act of regeneration; and through the continued work of sanctification he prepares them for their holy and happy abodes. Then he comes at death, when the mansions are fully prepared for the souls and the souls for the mansions, and takes each soul in its due time to be with him.

With this truth, and with all the scriptural teaching in reference to the glorious world which we have exhibited, a chastened imagination may follow departing saints from their earthly tenements amid a brighter atmosphere than that which darkens the German verses which we quoted at the beginning of our book.

Liberated from the confining trammels of earthly bodies, they are swiftly carried by angels aloft through "clouds of glory to the heaven of heavens."

As they enter the pearly gate a host of the unfallen creatures who rejoiced over their conversion greet them, and sing hallelujahs for their safe arrival.

A guard of honor escorts them to the throne on which is seated the great Judge, who declares their everlasting acceptance and ravishes them with the declaration, "Thou hast been faithful unto death; I now give thee a crown of life. Enter thou into the joy of thy Lord."

Redeemed friends who had gone before them welcome them with a joyous chorus. The Christian father or mother who was taken from one in the days of his youth; of another the child who was cut down as a flower, and the lock of whose silken hair was so tenderly kept in a well-guarded drawer; the wife who drooped and fell from her partner's side; or the husband whose supporting arm was suddenly paralyzed and his form laid in an untimely grave; the friends with whom sweet converse was often held, but the bond with whom was severed by the angel of death, —all who died in the faith meet them again before the great white throne, and with joy accompany them to their beautiful and blissful mansions. They inquire with eagerness as to the course of events in their circles on earth since their departure, and of the progress of the Church of Christ in the great work of subduing the world. And they tell, in heaven's language, of their experience in the glorious land, and of the riches of knowledge which they have already acquired from its older inhabitants.

From their communings with reunited friends the newly-arrived souls go forth with burning zeal to the public praise of the temple, and to the active life to which the Lord calls them.

Their mansions are gladdened by the presence of Him whose look makes heaven, and who shall make them live for ever in "tremulous waves of joy."

Thus the gracious life of earth purifies and expands itself into the glorious life of heaven.

Alternations of public service and private meditation; the clear study of the past and the piercing look away through eternity and infinity; outside activities and restful contemplation and mutual intercourse; public life and home life,—make up the one holy and happy existence in the FATHER'S HOUSE.

CHAPTER IX.

CONCLUSION.

THE exhibition of this most delightful subject has at every step presented truths which possess a comforting and practical power upon the heart. From beginning to end it is full of consolation and of an inspiring influence. But, in addition, we shall close our little book with direct appeals to three classes of readers.

1. Has death removed Christian friends from you? Think not of them as dead, nor even as asleep in some obscure place that you know nothing about, but as living in the most beautiful part of God's universe, with Jesus and all the blessed, and in the

enjoyment of a happiness which it is beyond our power adequately to express, which we can indeed scarcely conceive. And so live, in view of your own death, as to be able to adopt these exceedingly touching words:

"If death my friend and me divide,
Thou dost not, Lord, my sorrow chide,
Or frown my tears to see;
Restrained from passionate excess,
Thou bid'st me mourn in calm distress
For her that rests in thee.

"I feel a strong immortal hope
Which bears my mournful spirit up
Beneath its mountain load;
Redeemed from death and grief and pain,
I soon shall find my friend again
Within the arms of God.

"Pass a few fleeting moments more,
And death the blessing will restore
Which death has snatched away;
For me thou wilt the summons send,
And give me back my parted friend
In heaven's eternal day."

2. If you are a Christian, live above the dread of death. A sting there still is in

this penalty of sin, but it is soon withdrawn. This Jordan is a wildly rushing stream, but the crossing is quickly made; and then the bliss! Jesus has passed over it before you; an innumerable multitude of spirits made perfect have also gone through it, and just on the other side of it they are waiting to receive your soul as it is borne by angels to the presence of the glorious One. Be faithful unto death. Make the most of the time that still remains on earth to increase your treasures of grace in heaven. Whatever talent has been given to you, whatever opportunity of usefulness is afforded to you, employ it liberally for God. Make five, ten, twenty, a hundred, out of it if you can, knowing that accordingly your gracious and glorious reward shall be five, ten, twenty, a hundred, times as great. When the happiness of heaven is so varied and so multiplying, and is so connected with our activity, can any one be satisfied with merely getting in the gate? Work for God. If it is sometimes a toil and weariness to do it, remember that there is an eternity of rest. Strive manfully against sins, even against the most cherished ones. Seek to bring heaven down to earth now in your character and in your life. Patiently, calmly, submissively, bear the trials which the Father may send upon you. Then the more sufferings you pass through, the more weary you become and the older you grow in this world of strife and pain and corruption, the nearer will come to you such words as these:

"I'm kneeling at the threshold, weary, faint and sore,
Waiting for the dawning, for the opening of the door;
Waiting till the Master shall bid me rise and come
To the glory of his presence, to the gladness of his home.

"A weary path I've traveled, 'mid darkness, storm and strife,
Bearing many a burden, struggling for my life;
But now the morn is breaking, my toil will soon be o'er;
I'm kneeling at the threshold, my hand is on the door.

"Methinks I hear the voices of the blessèd as they stand
Singing in the sunshine of the sinless land;
Oh, would that I were with them, amid their shining throng,
Mingling in their worship, joining in their song!

"The friends that started with me have entered long ago;
One by one they left me struggling with the foe;
Their pilgrimage was shorter, their triumph sooner won;
How lovingly they'll hail me when my toil is done!

"With them the blessèd angels, that know nor grief nor sin,
I see them by the portals prepared to let me in.
O Lord, I wait thy pleasure—thy time and way are best;
But I'm wasted, worn and weary; O Father, bid me rest!"*

And when the summons of the Father comes you will enter upon the joy and the glory of the following description:

"At length the door is opened, and free from pain and sin,
With joy and gladness on his head, the pilgrim enters in;
The Master bids him welcome, and on the Father's breast,
By loving arms enfolded, the weary is at rest.

* These yearning verses appeared originally in the *Sunday Magazine*, vol. i., p. 352, under the title of "The Aged Believer at the Gate of Heaven." We have seen them more than once quoted as the production of Dr. Guthrie, who was then the editor of that periodical; but the initials appended to them, "W. L. A.," belong to the Rev. W. L. Alexander, D. D., who supplemented them by the other little poem we have quoted, which he published in the same magazine, vol. iii., p. 372, under the title, "The Aged Saint entering Heaven." Perhaps it is not as widely known as the former. We think it even more beautiful and enrapturing than the first one in some respects, especially for aged saints; and have therefore added it.

"The pilgrim's staff is left behind, behind the sword, the shield,
The armor dimmed and dinted on many a hard-fought field;
His now the shining palace, the garden of delight,
The palm, the robe, the diadem, the glory ever bright.

"The blessèd angels round him, 'mid heaven's hallowed calm,
With harp and voice are lifting up the triumph of their psalm:
'All glory to the holy One, the infinite I AM,
Whose grace redeems the fallen! Salvation to the Lamb!

"'Another son of Adam's race, through Jesu's loving might,
Hath crossed the waste, hath reached the goal, hath vanquished in the fight:
Hail, brother, hail! we welcome thee! join in our sweet accord,
Lift up the burden of our song, Salvation to the Lord!'

"And now from out the glory, the living cloud of light,
The old familiar faces come beaming on his sight;
The early lost, the ever loved, the friends of long ago,
Companions of his conflicts and pilgrimage below.

"They parted here in weakness, and suffering, and gloom;
They meet amid the freshness of heaven's immortal bloom,
Henceforth in ever-during bliss to wander, hand in hand,
Beside the living waters of the still and sinless land.

"Oh, who can tell the rapture of those to whom 'tis given
Thus to renew the bonds of earth amid the bliss of heaven?
Thrice blessèd be His holy name who for our fallen race
Hath purchased by his bitter pains such plenitude of grace."

3. Are any who read these pages unconverted? If the soul ceases not to exist

when the body dies; if it never becomes unconscious for a single instant; if it passes from the body with the mental and moral habits which it has acquired here in full and even increased activity: then, reader, if you be not changed by the power of God's Spirit, if the atoning blood of Jesus, received by faith, do not wash away your guilt, if a holy principle be not implanted in you and be not active in putting away evil habits and forming good ones, behold your dangerous condition! Should you thus die, into heaven you could not enter. With God you could not dwell. The society of the saved you could not enjoy. Therefore turn to the Lord. Remembering that the sooner you enter upon the narrow path, and the more fervent your zeal and the greater your activity for God in it, the more thorough will be your education for the heavenly service and the greater your preparation for its glorious joy, at once breathe the prayer of faith,

"Lord, remember me when thou comest into thy kingdom," and commence earnestly to live the Christian life, so that whensoever the messenger of death comes to you, be it suddenly or through the slow march of disease, be it with warning or without, your soul may receive from Jesus, with an abundant richness for which the dying penitent was not prepared, the sweet assurance,

"TO-DAY SHALT THOU BE WITH ME IN PARADISE."

www.ingramcontent.com/pod-product-compliance
Lightning Source LLC
LaVergne TN
LVHW011204110826
845150LV00006B/1313

* 9 7 8 1 4 2 5 5 1 8 8 1 3 *